Carbon Abatement Costs and Climate Change Finance

Carbon Abatement Costs and Climate Change Finance

William R. Cline

PETERSON INSTITUTE FOR INTERNATIONAL ECONOMICS
Washington, DC

July 2011

William R. Cline has been a senior fellow at the Peterson Institute for International Economics since its inception in 1981 and has held a joint appointment at the Center for Global Development since 2002. During 1996–2001 while on leave from the Institute, he was deputy managing director and chief economist of the Institute of International Finance. He is the author of 23 books, most recently *Financial Globalization, Economic Growth, and the Crisis of 2007–09* (2010). He was senior fellow, Brookings Institution (1973–81); deputy director of development and trade research, US Treasury Department (1971–73); Ford Foundation visiting professor in Brazil (1970–71); and lecturer and assistant professor of economics at Princeton University (1967–70).

PETER G. PETERSON INSTITUTE FOR INTERNATIONAL ECONOMICS
1750 Massachusetts Avenue, NW
Washington, DC 20036-1903
(202) 328-9000   FAX: (202) 659-3225
www.piie.com

C. Fred Bergsten, *Director*
Edward A. Tureen, *Director of Publications, Marketing, and Web Development*

Typesetting by Susann Luetjen
Printing by Versa Press, Inc.

Printed in the United States of America
12 11 10   5 4 3 2 1

Library of Congress Cataloging-in-Publication Data
Cline, William R.
  Carbon abatement costs and climate change finance / William R. Cline.
    p. cm.
  Includes bibliographical references and index.
  ISBN 978-0-88132-607-9
  1. Carbon offsetting. 2. Carbon dioxide mitigation—Costs. 3. Climatic changes—Economic aspects. 4. Global warming—International cooperation. I. Title.

  HC79.A4C5495 2011
  363.438'746—dc23

                                   2011017671

Contents

Preface ix

Acknowledgments xiii

1 Overview 1
   Policy Context 1
   Method and Plan of the Study 2
   Principal Findings 3

2 Baseline Emissions under Business as Usual 7
   Framework 7
   Decomposing Emissions Trends, 1990–2006 9
   Baseline through 2030 12
   Extending the Baseline through 2050 16

3 Abatement Initiatives in the Copenhagen Accord
   and Cancún Agreements 19
   Copenhagen Accord Pledges 20
   Cancún Agreements 23

4 Abatement Cost Functions 25
   Top-Down and Bottom-Up Models 25
   RICE Model 26
   EMF 22 Models 27
   McKinsey Model 30

5 Abatement Costs through 2050   **33**
Copenhagen Convergence   34
Abatement Costs under the Copenhagen Convergence Scenario   39
Other Model–Based Estimates   48
Alternative Abatement Paths   50

6 Trade and Timing   **57**
Shadow Price of Carbon Dioxide   58

7 Estimating Investment Requirements and Adaptation Costs   **71**
International Energy Agency   72
World Bank   74
Investment Levels Implied by Abatement Cost Estimates   75
Adaptation   79

8 Synthesis   **81**
The $100 Billion Copenhagen Commitment   81
Estimates of This Study   83

Appendices
Appendix A   Data Sources and Further Statistical Tables   91
Appendix B   Estimating Atmospheric CO_2 Concentrations under Alternative Emissions Paths   99
Appendix C   Other Greenhouse Gases and Aerosols   103
Appendix D   Alternative Policy Paths for CO_2 Emissions, 2010–50   107
Appendix E   Abatement Costs of the Alternative Policy Paths   113
Appendix F   Cost-Minimizing Reallocation of Abatement over Time   117
Appendix G   Abatement Cost Function Estimates Based on EMF 22   121

References   **131**

Index   **135**

Tables
Table 2.1   Carbon dioxide emissions: Growth decomposition, 1990–2006   10
Table 2.2   Business as usual baseline emissions of carbon dioxide   13
Table 2.3   Decomposition of emissions growth, 2010–20   14
Table 2.4   Decomposition of emissions growth, 2020–30   15
Table 2.5   Business as usual baseline, 2030–50   17
Table 3.1   Country targets and initiatives under the Copenhagen Accord   21
Table 4.1   Multiplicative abatement cost parameter (α) in the Nordhaus RICE model   27

Table 4.2	Abatement cost function parameters, EMF 22 synthesis model	28
Table 4.3	Ackerman et al. abatement cost parameters from McKinsey for 2030	31
Table 5.1	Business as usual baseline and Copenhagen Convergence target emissions, 2020 and 2050	37
Table 5.2	Business as usual baseline and Copenhagen Convergence abatement path: Annual rates of growth in carbon plus energy efficiency	38
Table 5.3	Percent reduction in emissions from business as usual baseline, Copenhagen Convergence scenario	40
Table 5.4	Abatement costs for the Copenhagen Convergence policy path: RICE model basis	41
Table 5.5	Abatement costs for the Copenhagen Convergence policy path: EMF 22 synthesis model basis	44
Table 5.6	Abatement costs in 2030 for the Copenhagen Convergence policy path: McKinsey/Ackerman et al. basis	47
Table 5.7	2050 emissions under Copenhagen Convergence and UNDP scenarios	54
Table 5.8	Cumulative CO_2 emissions after 2010 and atmospheric concentrations	55
Table 6.1	Shadow price of CO_2 under Copenhagen Convergence abatement in the absence of international offsets trading	60
Table 6.2	Purchases or sales of CO_2 emissions rights, global shadow price, and savings from emissions trading: RICE cost function basis	64
Table 6.3	Global CO_2 emissions under alternative variants of the Copenhagen Convergence policy scenario	67
Table 6.4	Present value of abatement costs under alternative Copenhagen Convergence scenarios: RICE cost basis	69
Table 7.1	Annual investment required for Copenhagen Convergence abatement, 2020–40	77
Table 8.1	Abatement costs for the Copenhagen Convergence policy path	84
Table 8.2	Developing-country financing needs for abatement and adaptation and financial flows from offset purchases	85
Table A.1	Population	92
Table A.2	Baseline per capita GDP	94
Table A.3	Business as usual baseline CO_2 emissions per capita	96
Table A.4	Business as usual baseline energy consumption	97
Table C.1	Radiative forcing of other greenhouse gases and aerosols by 2050 under business as usual low scenario B1p	104
Table D.1	CO_2 emissions path under Copenhagen Convergence scenario	108
Table D.2	CO_2 emissions path under UNDP (2007)	109

Table D.3 CO_2 emissions path under Chakravarty et al. (2009)   110
Table D.4 CO_2 emissions path under Frankel (2008)   111
Table E.1   Abatement costs: UNDP (2007)   113
Table E.2   Abatement costs: Chakravarty et al. (2009)   115
Table E.3   Abatement costs: Frankel (2008)   116
Table F.1   Emissions profile under cost-minimization discounting   118
             at 1.5 percent per year
Table F.2   Emissions profile under cost-minimization discounting   119
             at 3 percent per year
Table F.3   Emissions profile under cost-minimization discounting   120
             at 5 percent per year
Table G.1   Regression results for abatement cost function   124
Table G.2   Abatement costs for the Copenhagen Convergence   127
             policy path: EMF 22 synthesis model basis constrained
Table G.3   Investment required for Copenhagen Convergence   129
             abatement: 2020 and 2030

Figures

Figure 4.1   Comparison of RICE and EMF 22 based abatement   29
             cost estimates for uniform cuts from baseline
Figure 5.1   Business as usual and Copenhagen Convergence   36
             abatement emissions paths, 1990–2050
Figure 5.2   Alternative policy paths for CO_2 emissions, 2010–50   53
Figure B.1   Business as usual emissions and increased atmospheric   100
             concentrations: SRES scenario estimates and regression
             equation
Figure G.1   Abatement cost with purchases of emissions rights   126

Preface

In this study, William Cline continues his work on climate change that began with his path-breaking 1992 book, *The Economics of Global Warming*, and includes his most recent book *Global Warming and Agriculture: Impact Estimates by Country* (2007). This new analysis focuses on the abatement costs likely to be required to keep global warming within the internationally endorsed ceiling of 2°C warming above preindustrial temperatures. Cline employs three leading abatement cost models to examine a "Copenhagen Convergence" policy scenario in which the major nations achieve their 2020 emissions curbs pledged at Copenhagen in December 2009 and thereafter converge to uniform low per capita emissions by 2050.

The momentum for action on greenhouse gas abatement has faltered recently, at least in the United States with the failure of Senate action on legislation on emissions restraint after the Waxman-Markey bill passed the House of Representatives in 2009. The estimates in this study should provide some reassurance that forceful action is possible without imposing prohibitive economic costs. The central model estimates indicate that abatement costs would amount to about one-third to two-thirds of one percent of GDP for industrial countries by 2030 and moderately less for developing countries. But participation of the major emerging-market economies will be necessary for success and by 2050 the cutbacks from the business-as-usual baseline for China and some others among them are surprisingly close to the deep cuts in industrial countries—because of the rapid rise of emissions otherwise associated with rapid growth.

The Institute has sought to contribute to the debate on the new international economic architecture needed to curb global warming. In 2008, the Institute published *Leveling the Carbon Playing Field* by Visiting Fellow Trevor

Houser and coauthors from the World Resources Institute. Senior Fellows Gary Hufbauer and Jeffrey Schott have written working papers on World Trade Organization (WTO) rules relating to climate change and the prospects for US-NAFTA cooperation on abatement, and Hufbauer, Steve Charnovitz, and Jisun Kim published a major book in 2009 entitled *Global Warming and the World Trading System*.

The Peter G. Peterson Institute for International Economics is a private, nonprofit institution for the study and discussion of international economic policy. Its purpose is to analyze important issues in that area and to develop and communicate practical new approaches for dealing with them. The Institute is completely nonpartisan.

The Institute is funded by a highly diversified group of philanthropic foundations, private corporations, and interested individuals. About 35 percent of the Institute's resources in our latest fiscal year was provided by contributors outside the United States. The Doris Duke Charitable Foundation has provided generous support for much of the Institute's recent work on climate change, including the present study. In 2009–10 the Foundation provided support to focus on developing countries' financing needs for climate action. The present study translates the abatement cost estimates into prospective financing needs (chapter 7), including for adaptation. It turns out that the benchmark Copenhagen Accord figure of $100 billion annually by 2020 is broadly supported by the calculations developed here.

The Institute's Board of Directors bears overall responsibilities for the Institute and gives general guidance and approval to its research program, including the identification of topics that are likely to become important over the medium run (one to three years) and that should be addressed by the Institute. The director, working closely with the staff and outside Advisory Committee, is responsible for the development of particular projects and makes the final decision to publish an individual study.

The Institute hopes that its studies and other activities will contribute to building a stronger foundation for international economic policy around the world. We invite readers of these publications to let us know how they think we can best accomplish this objective.

C. FRED BERGSTEN
Director
June 2011

x

Acknowledgments

I thank Thomas Emmons and Yimei Zou for painstaking and inspired research assistance. For comments on an earlier draft, I thank without implicating Trevor Houser, Caio Koch-Weser, and an anonymous reviewer.

1

Overview

The major nations have come tantalizingly close to beginning more meaningful action to curb global warming. The Copenhagen Accord of December 2009, ratified and more formally incorporated into the United Nations climate negotiations system at Cancún, Mexico, in December 2010, set a target of limiting warming to 2°C above preindustrial levels. For the first time, the Copenhagen Accord took the crucial step of incorporating the major developing countries into an international action program. The sole previous (and still extant) internationally agreed mechanism, the Kyoto Protocol, was incapable of meaningfully curbing global warming because its limits on emissions applied only to industrial countries, yet the share of these countries in global emissions is already slightly less than half and under business as usual will shrink to less than 40 percent by 2030 and about 30 percent by 2050 (tables 2.2 and 2.5 in chapter 2).

Policy Context

The eventual damages from unrestrained global warming could be severe. With 3°C warming by late in this century, agricultural production potential would fall by 3 to 16 percent globally, 17 to 28 percent in Africa, 29 to 38 percent in India, 20 to 30 percent in Pakistan, 9 to 21 percent in the Middle East and North Africa, and 13 to 24 percent in Latin America, depending on whether "carbon fertilization" benefits partially offset heat stress (Cline 2007, pp. 69, 96). With even 2°C warming, on a time scale of centuries, the Greenland ice cap would likely melt, raising sea level 7 meters. With considerably higher warming and on a time scale of millennia, sea levels could rise 60 to 80 meters, the oceans become anoxic from shutdown of the ocean conveyor belt, and anaerobic bacteria emit hydrogen sulfide in toxic amounts, a mechanism that may have caused the Permian-Triassic mass extinction 251 million years ago (Cline

2011, Kump et al. 2005). Stakes and time scales such as these bedevil fine-point calculations of optimal abatement and argue for an insurance approach that focuses on even small probabilities of disastrous impacts (Weitzman 2007).

The central policy questions then become: How expensive is insurance against global warming, and who will pay the insurance policy premiums? This study seeks to examine the prospective costs of abatement through 2050 at the global level and in detail for the 25 largest economies (with the European Union treated as a single economy). It also attempts to shed light on the magnitude of abatement investment requirements and adaptation costs in developing countries by 2020 and to relate them to the target of $100 billion in international support pledged by industrial countries in the Copenhagen Accord.

Method and Plan of the Study

Chapter 2 sets forth a framework for evaluating prospective economic costs of reducing carbon dioxide emissions in the context of a coordinated international effort to curb global warming. The framework first identifies the business as usual (bau) emissions baseline for each of the 25 largest emitting economies. These baselines are examined as a function of four parameters: population growth, growth of per capita GDP, growth in the "energy efficiency of output" (inverse of energy required per unit of GDP), and growth in the "carbon efficiency of energy" (inverse of carbon dioxide emissions per unit of energy). Actual trends in these influences are estimated for the period 1990–2006. Prospective bau baseline trends for these parameters for each of the next four decades are then identified, taking into account such existing projections as those of the Energy Information Administration (EIA 2009) and the various emissions paths considered by the Intergovernmental Panel on Climate Change (IPCC 2001).

Chapter 3 reviews the emissions policy pledges undertaken by major countries in the Copenhagen Accord for the period through 2020 and the subsequent Cancún Agreements. Chapter 4 sets forth three leading abatement cost models (or in one case, family of models) that serve as the basis for the study's cost calculations.[1] Chapter 5 then identifies the policy paths for cuts from the bau baseline. These cutbacks determine the abatement costs in the cost models applied. The principal policy scenario is a Copenhagen Convergence scenario built around the abatement initiatives undertaken in Copenhagen. Reductions from bau baselines by 2020 are estimated for the Accord, which includes pledges by 14 of the 25 large emitting economies. For the United States and the European Union, pledges were also made for reductions by 2050. The central policy scenario postulates straight-line reductions from 2020 levels to a 2050 target of uniform per capita emissions level of 1.43 tons of carbon dioxide per year, broadly consistent with the objective of limiting atmospheric concentra-

---

1. The RICE model developed by William Nordhaus (2010b); those of McKinsey (2009) as compiled by Ackerman et al. (2010); and specially estimated equations based on model results compiled in Energy Modeling Forum 22 (see appendix G).

tion to 450 parts per million (ppm) and limiting global warming to 2°C.[2] To check compatibility with this objective, a summary formula is developed for relating cumulative emissions to atmospheric concentration of carbon dioxide (appendix B). The analysis next calculates costs that would be associated with this central global abatement policy scenario. Alternative policy scenarios are also considered (appendix D).[3]

In chapter 6 the efficiency of abatement is examined further for the Copenhagen Convergence scenario. The marginal cost of abatement for each country and each period is calculated for the scenario. A cost minimization exercise is then conducted in which countries are allowed to trade emissions rights subject to the constraint that total global abatement for the year in question remains unchanged. Further scope for cost minimization is then examined through allowing reallocation of emissions cutbacks across time in the four decades and under alternative discount rate assumptions.

Chapter 7 turns to implications for international climate finance. A method is proposed for converting abatement cost estimates into corresponding investment requirements, based on the relationship between capital stock and output flows of magnitudes capable of compensating for the abatement cost impacts. Investment requirements are then estimated applying this method to the range of abatement cost estimates. For developing countries, these investment requirements are compared with the benchmark figure of $100 billion per year in financing by 2020 endorsed by industrial countries in the Copenhagen Accord. As this amount is meant to include costs of adaptation to warming not avoided, the analysis also considers the range of adaptation costs. The discussion also considers the role of "carbon offset" payments, whereby industrial-country firms purchase emissions reductions in developing countries as a means of meeting emissions limits, in relationship to the benchmark financing total. Chapter 8 provides a synthesis of the estimates of the study.

Principal Findings

Among the most important findings of this study are the following:

- The Copenhagen pledges for 2020 would cut global carbon dioxide emissions by 9 percent from the bau baseline, from 35.9 to 32.7 billion tons of carbon dioxide (GtCO$_2$).

---

2. This path would require somewhat deeper cuts for the European Union and United States by 2050 than the two offered in their Copenhagen Accord submissions. Note also that the Copenhagen Convergence scenario limits concentrations by 2050 to somewhat less than 450 ppm for carbon dioxide alone, but somewhat more for CO$_2$-equivalent of all greenhouse gases, as discussed later.

3. These include the influential proposal by the United Nations Development Program (UNDP 2007) as well as two leading proposals by academic researchers (Chakravarty et al. 2009, Frankel 2008). Using the RICE model cost parameters, a range of abatement costs corresponding to the range of policy scenarios is explored.

- To achieve a path limiting warming to 2°C and atmospheric concentrations of CO_2 to 450 ppm, it will be necessary to cut 2050 emissions from a baseline of 53.2 to 13.3 $GtCO_2$ (a reduction of 75 percent from baseline) (table 5.1 in chapter 5).

- In 1990–2006, efficiency of output relative to energy use rose at 1.4 percent annually for the 25 largest economies, while energy efficiency per unit of carbon required did not grow at all. From 2010 to 2030, baseline EIA projections indicate 2 percent annual output/energy efficiency growth but again zero energy/carbon efficiency growth. To achieve the needed emissions cuts from 2020 to 2050, it will be necessary for the sum of these two efficiency growth rates to reach 6 percent annually (table 5.2). Most of this acceleration likely will need to come from a shift to carbon-spare or carbon-free energy.

- To mobilize global political support for abatement, particularly in developing countries, it would be appropriate after 2020 to pursue international convergence to uniform per capita emissions by 2050. The required 2050 level would be 1.43 tons of carbon dioxide (tCO_2) per person, compared with today's levels of 19.3 tons in the United States, 5.0 tons in China, and 1.4 tons in India.

- This Copenhagen Convergence path would be only modestly more ambitious than the 2050 cutbacks of 80 percent from 1990 levels pledged at Copenhagen by the European Union and 83 percent from 2005 levels pledged by the United States (reaching, respectively, 84 and 89 percent from 1990 and 2005 levels).

- The 75 percent global cutback from bau baseline by 2050 would represent 89 percent cuts for industrial countries on average and 69 percent cuts for developing countries. Because of their rapid baseline growth in output and carbon, such emerging-market economies as China, Malaysia, South Africa, and South Korea would need to cut emissions by 85 to 90 percent from the 2050 baseline, surprisingly similar in depth to cuts needed by industrial countries.

- Despite these seemingly daunting cutbacks, on the basis of the leading abatement cost models it turns out that the costs would be modest. By 2030, in the prominent RICE model abatement costs would amount to about one-fourth of one percent of GDP (0.28 percent for industrial countries, 0.19 percent for developing countries); by 2050 the RICE-based estimate reaches 1.2 percent of world product (1.6 percent industrial countries, 1.0 percent developing countries; table 5.4). Costs in the leading bottom-up model (McKinsey) are considerably lower. Costs are somewhat higher in a family of regional cost functions estimated from results of the Stanford Energy Modeling Forum (EMF) 22 model survey, but not radically so. In the preferred variant, the EMF 22–based costs by 2030 amount to 0.67 percent of GDP for industrial countries and 0.62 percent for developing countries (table G.2 in appendix G).

- Abatement costs can be limited further by international emissions trade, and by shifting cutbacks earlier in time, toward a more aggressive target by 2020 than the Copenhagen pledges. The present value of abatement costs over the next 40 years amounts to 0.45 percent of world product (discounting at 1.5 percent, and less if higher discount rates are used). If emissions trading is allowed and marginal costs are equalized across countries, the present value of abatement costs falls to 0.40 percent. If in addition the cutbacks are moved forward in time, especially in China, where there are no cutbacks yet from baseline by 2020, the present value of abatement costs can be further reduced to 0.33 percent of the present value of world product over the four decades (table 6.4 in chapter 6).

- The global carbon dioxide price that emerges when trading is allowed stands at $54 per ton of carbon dioxide in 2030 (in 2005 dollars, RICE model cost-function basis), in the same range as the $40 per ton of carbon dioxide "allowance" price estimated by the US Congressional Budget Office for US abatement under the Waxman-Markey bill passed by the House of Representatives in 2009 (table 6.2).

- Based on a simple model relating capital stock to output, the annual investment needed to create economic capacity providing output equal to offset abatement costs would stand at about 40 percent of the annual abatement cost magnitude (rather than two to three times as high as implied in some recent official studies). Translation of the estimated abatement costs in developing countries using this approach into corresponding annual investment yields a total of $53 billion in China and $41 billion in other developing countries by 2020 and, respectively, $176 billion and $118 billion by 2030 (table 8.2 in chapter 8).[4]

- The main estimates of adaptation costs (for such measures as coastal protection and response to increased malaria threat) place these at about $40 billion annually by 2020 and $50 billion by 2030. Together, and excluding China (with the world's largest foreign exchange reserves) as not needing international financing, the abatement investment costs plus adaptation costs sum to about $80 billion for 2020, on the same order of magnitude as the $100 billion Copenhagen pledge (and without counting offset purchases).

The broad implication of the estimates of this study is that that although the costs and financing requirements for aggressive international action limiting climate change will be substantial, they should be of a sufficiently manageable magnitude that the outcome is likely to depend more on political will rather than economic feasibility.

---

4. Investment would be needed already by 2020 in China despite no change from baseline in that year in order to set on track the abatement needed during 2020–30 to follow the Copenhagen Convergence path. The abatement cost estimate used as the basis for the investment calculation is the average of the estimates from the RICE model and the preferred variant of the EMF 22 estimates.

2

Baseline Emissions under Business as Usual

In models of abatement cost, the driving force in the calculations is typically the depth of the emissions cut from a business as usual (bau) baseline. The first step in this study is thus to estimate bau emissions through 2050. The estimates are developed for the world as a whole and at the country level for the 25 largest emitting economies (with the European Union treated as a single country). A decomposition framework useful for this purpose distinguishes four influences determining emissions growth: rising population, rising per capita GDP, trends in efficiency in energy use per unit of GDP, and trends in carbon-saving increases in energy per unit of carbon emitted. For 25 economies accounting for 92 percent of global emissions in 2007, emissions rose at an annual rate of 1.8 percent from 1990 to 2006, composed of 1 percent for population growth, 2 percent for per capita output growth, offset by 1.4 percent annual increase in output efficiency of energy, with virtually no change in efficiency of carbon usage of energy.

Baseline projections through 2030 are taken from the Energy Information Administration. They show that by 2030 China alone will have approximately the same emissions as the United States, European Union, and Japan combined. The projections are extended through 2050 by applying projections of population growth and extrapolations of the 2020–30 country-specific growth rates of per capita output, energy efficiency, and carbon efficiency. The resulting global totals by 2050 amount to 53 billion tons of carbon dioxide ($GtCO_2$), in the same broad range as a key scenario used by the Intergovernmental Panel on Climate Change (IPCC): "A2," with 61 $GtCO_2$ by 2050.

Framework

For any of the major emitting countries, let E_t = emissions of carbon dioxide (excluding from deforestation, not considered in the present study) in year t.

Let N_t = population in year t. Let q_t = real GDP per capita, at 2005 constant international purchasing power parity (ppp) dollars. Let λ_t = output per unit of energy, or "energy efficiency." Let γ_t = energy per unit of carbon dioxide, or "carbon efficiency." Referring to constant rates over a period of a decade, for the decade and country in question the path of population will follow:

$$N_t = N_0 e^{nt} \tag{2.1}$$

where n is the rate of growth of population, subscript 0 denotes the year at the beginning of the decade, and e is the base of the natural logarithm. Similarly, output per capita will follow the path:

$$q_t = q_0 e^{gt} \tag{2.2}$$

where g is the growth rate of per capita income. Total production will then equal:

$$Q_t = N_t q_t \tag{2.3}$$

Total carbon dioxide emissions will then equal total output divided by the energy efficiency parameter (output per unit of energy) times the carbon efficiency parameter (energy per unit of carbon), or:

$$E_t = \frac{Q_t}{\lambda_t \gamma_t} \tag{2.4}$$

The time path for the energy and carbon efficiency parameters, in turn, will be:

$$\lambda_t = \lambda_0 e^{wt} \tag{2.5}$$

and

$$\gamma_t = \gamma_0 e^{ct} \tag{2.6}$$

where w is the annual rate of increase in energy efficiency of output and c is the annual rate of increase in carbon efficiency of energy.

Substituting, the time path for carbon dioxide emissions will be:

$$
\begin{aligned}
E_t &= \frac{N_0 e^{nt} q_0 e^{gt}}{\lambda_0 e^{wt} \gamma_0 e^{ct}} \\
&= \frac{N_0 q_0}{\lambda_0 \gamma_0} e^{(n+g-w-c)t} = E_0 e^{(n+g-w-c)t}
\end{aligned}
\tag{2.7}
$$

The annual rate of change of emissions will then be the ratio of the derivative of this expression to the expression itself:

$$\dot{E}_t = \frac{dE_t/dt}{E_t} = \frac{(n+g-w-c)E_0 e^{(n+g-w-c)t}}{E_0 e^{(n+g-w-c)t}} = n + g - w - c \tag{2.8}$$

So it turns out that the rate of growth of emissions for the country and decade in question will simply equal the period growth rate of population plus the growth rate of per capita GDP minus the growth rate of the energy efficiency of output minus the growth rate of the carbon efficiency of energy.

Decomposing Emissions Trends, 1990–2006

The framework in equations 2.1 to 2.8 can be used to decompose the growth of carbon dioxide emissions from fossil fuels (and hence excluding deforestation) by major emitting nations in recent decades. Table 2.1 reports this decomposition.

The six largest emitters in 2006 were China, the United States, the European Union, Russia, India, and Japan. Emissions growth rates for 1990–2006 were high in China and India, intermediate in the United States, and low in the European Union, Japan, and Russia. High emissions growth in China reflected very high growth in per capita GDP and low (negative) growth in carbon efficiency of energy (c), which more than offset high growth in energy efficiency of output (w). In this respect it is encouraging that China has announced its intention to reduce the carbon intensity of GDP by 40 to 45 percent by 2020 (as discussed below). In the 2006–10 five-year plan, China instead solely emphasized increased energy efficiency.[1] In India, rapid emissions growth reflected high demographic expansion, high growth in GDP per capita, and substantial negative growth in carbon efficiency of energy, which together more than offset relatively high growth in energy efficiency of output.

Low growth of emissions in Japan reflected low population growth and only moderate economic growth and was achieved despite low growth in energy efficiency of output (albeit from an already high base). In Russia, carbon dioxide emissions declined by about one-fourth from 1990 to 2006 as a consequence of a decline in GDP and increase in output efficiency of energy (but only to a still low level of λ by 2006). Intermediate emissions growth in the United States reflected intermediate population and economic growth only partially offset by relatively rapid energy efficiency growth, with virtually no change in carbon efficiency of energy.

For the 25 major emitting countries (including the European Union as one), emissions rose at 1.82 percent annually from 1990 to 2006. The largest source of emissions growth was from per capita output growth (about 2.1 percent). Population growth added about 1.1 percent per year, but rising energy efficiency of output provided an offset of about 1.4 percent per year. There was almost no contribution at all to emissions restraint from the source of carbon efficiency of energy (–0.03 percent per year).

---

1. For the 2006–10 five-year plan, China pledged to reduce energy use per unit of GDP by 20 percent. This amounted to a pace of 3.7 percent per year, compared with 4.8 percent achieved in 1990–2006 (table 2.1).

Table 2.1   Carbon dioxide emissions: Growth decomposition, 1990–2006[a]

Country/economy	Level, 2006 (million metric tons)	Growth rates, 1990–2006 (annual percent)					Efficiency parameters, 2006[b]	
		Total	n	g	w	c	λ	γ
Argentina	173	2.70	1.13	2.76	1.36	-0.17	6.66	0.40
Australia	372	1.48	1.18	1.98	1.07	0.60	5.38	0.33
Brazil	352	3.27	1.48	1.23	-0.51	-0.05	7.47	0.64
Canada	544	1.19	1.01	1.75	1.18	0.39	4.32	0.50
China	6,099	5.79	0.84	8.84	4.82	-0.93	3.16	0.31
Egypt	167	4.91	1.87	2.20	-0.13	-0.71	5.37	0.37
European Union	4,050	-0.23	0.22	1.96	1.57	0.83	7.17	0.45
India	1,509	4.89	1.74	4.33	2.51	-1.32	4.73	0.37
Indonesia	333	4.97	1.52	2.96	1.03	-1.53	4.32	0.54
Iran	467	4.50	0.86	2.76	-2.07	1.19	3.70	0.37
Japan	1,293	0.61	0.20	1.12	0.24	0.47	7.50	0.41
Kazakhstan	193	-1.88	-0.46	1.85	2.52	0.75	2.36	0.32
Malaysia	188	7.49	2.07	3.80	-0.84	-0.78	4.36	0.36
Mexico	436	0.78	1.47	1.59	0.77	1.51	7.89	0.41
Pakistan	143	4.57	2.28	1.89	0.41	-0.81	4.76	0.56
Russia	1,564	-1.77	-0.25	0.08	1.46	0.13	2.69	0.43
Saudi Arabia	381	3.58	3.25	0.73	-1.45	1.85	3.95	0.38
South Africa	414	1.36	1.38	0.78	-0.05	0.85	3.27	0.31

South Korea	475	4.22	0.72	4.63	0.10	1.03	5.31	0.46
Taiwan	273	4.82	0.73	4.52	0.43	-0.01	5.62	0.38
Thailand	272	6.53	0.99	3.60	-0.77	-1.17	4.19	0.38
Turkey	269	3.80	1.66	2.47	0.53	-0.21	9.09	0.35
Ukraine	319	-4.07	-0.64	-1.81	1.33	0.29	2.05	0.43
United States	5,748	1.04	1.10	1.81	1.75	0.12	5.49	0.40
Venezuela	171	2.12	1.77	0.73	0.32	0.06	4.44	0.36
25 emitters	26,207	1.82	1.09	2.06	1.36	-0.03	5.13	0.39

n = population; g = ppp GDP per capita; w = energy efficiency; c = carbon efficiency

a. Fossil fuels and cement; excludes deforestation.

b. Thousands of 2005 purchasing power parity (ppp) GDP dollars per ton oil equivalent (toe) and toe per tCO_2.

Source: See appendix A.

Baseline through 2030

The Energy Information Administration (EIA 2009) provides business as usual projections of emissions by major economy and region through 2030. Appendix A discusses the use of these projections as the primary basis for the bau baseline in the present study. Tables A.1 through A.4 report the corresponding projections of population, real GDP per capita (2005 ppp dollars), emissions per capita, and annual energy consumption.[2] Table 2.2 reports the resulting bau baseline estimates used in the present study. In the aggregates, Russia is included in the industrial-country subtotal.

In the bau baseline based on the EIA projections, global emissions rise from 29.5 GtCO$_2$ in 2007 to 41.4 GtCO$_2$ by 2030. The pace of emissions growth decelerates only marginally, from about 1.7 percent per year from 1990 to 2007 to about 1.5 percent in the coming decade and 1.4 percent in the 2020s. China's share in global emissions, which has risen from 11 percent in 1990 to 22.4 percent in 2007, rises further to 28.7 percent by 2030, or more than its share in global population at that time (17.7 percent; table A.1). In contrast, the share of the United States, the European Union, and Japan in global emissions, which stood at 46.7 percent in 1990 and had fallen to 37.7 percent by 2007, declines further to 28 percent by 2030—almost identical to the share of China alone.

Table A.4 in appendix A reports the EIA's projections of energy consumption through 2030 for regions and major economies. Given the projections of purchasing power parity per capita GDP, population, energy consumption, and emissions, it is possible to decompose emissions growth into the components discussed above (population, n; ppp per capita GDP, g; subtraction of energy efficiency growth, w; and subtraction of carbon efficiency growth, c). Tables 2.3 and 2.4 report these bau baseline decompositions for 2010–20 and 2020–30, respectively.[3]

Over the next two decades, continued high economic growth in China combines with the already high emissions base to drive the increase in the share of world emissions to about 30 percent. Even so, the projections allow for some deceleration in China's per capita growth: from 8.8 percent annually in 1990–2006 (table 2.1) to about 6 percent in the 2010s (table 2.3) and about 4 percent in the 2020s (table 2.4).

The components of emissions growth in tables 2.1, 2.3, and 2.4 do not show radical changes from one decade to the next. For the 25 major emit-

---

2. Specifically estimated by EIA for the largest economies and based on regional trends for others; see appendix A. Note that "European Union" in the table is for the 27 current members of the European Union. The EU estimate is calculated as the base level for 2007 for these countries specifically, and then for 2020 and 2030 it is based on the proportionate emissions growth for "OECD Europe" in the EIA projections.

3. Data for major industrial countries are from the EIA estimates. For countries without detailed estimates in the EIA source, the energy, economic growth, and emissions projections are based on averages for the regions in which the countries are located.

Table 2.2 Business as usual baseline emissions of carbon dioxide
(million metric tons)

Country/economy	Level				Annual percent growth	
	1990	2007	2020	2030	2007–20	2020–30
Argentina	113	172	207	225	1.42	0.84
Australia	293	377	401	433	0.49	0.76
Brazil	209	352	511	642	2.87	2.28
Canada	450	530	601	651	0.97	0.80
China	2,415	6,603	9,544	11,889	2.83	2.20
Egypt	76	192	210	239	0.71	1.29
European Union	4,200	4,050	4,070	4,133	0.04	0.15
India	691	1,574	2,083	2,471	2.15	1.71
Indonesia	150	416	475	633	1.01	2.88
Iran	227	476	621	730	2.05	1.62
Japan	1,172	1,236	1,264	1,199	0.17	−0.52
Kazakhstan	261	195	225	236	1.12	0.46
Malaysia	57	248	267	357	0.58	2.88
Mexico	385	445	471	563	0.44	1.78
Pakistan	69	148	203	271	2.41	2.88
Russia	2,075	1,585	1,785	1,815	0.91	0.17
Saudi Arabia	215	423	508	597	1.41	1.62
South Africa	334	434	523	595	1.44	1.29
South Korea	242	477	569	627	1.36	0.97
Taiwan	126	263	388	518	3.01	2.88
Thailand	96	309	388	517	1.75	2.88
Turkey	147	290	271	275	−0.53	0.15
Ukraine	612	321	372	389	1.12	0.46
United States	4,865	5,812	5,821	6,242	0.01	0.70
Venezuela	122	153	205	223	2.25	0.84
25 emitters	19,600	27,080	31,984	36,470	1.28	1.31
Rest of world industrial	301	522	515	541	−0.11	0.48
Rest of world developing	2,000	1,849	3,436	4,374	4.77	2.41
World	21,901	29,451	35,935	41,384	1.53	1.41
Industrial[a]	13,356	14,112	14,457	15,014	0.19	0.38
Developing	8,545	15,339	21,478	26,370	2.59	2.05

a. Includes Russia.

Source: See appendix A; author's calculations.

Table 2.3 Decomposition of emissions growth, 2010–20
(annual percent)

Country/economy	n	g	w	c	Emissions
Argentina	0.93	2.36	2.72	0.35	0.23
Australia	1.07	2.33	2.00	0.61	0.78
Brazil	1.02	2.73	1.34	0.23	2.17
Canada	0.75	1.60	1.13	0.41	0.82
China	0.60	6.15	3.60	0.50	2.65
Egypt	1.79	2.15	2.30	0.33	1.32
European Union	0.04	2.00	1.37	0.41	0.26
India	1.23	4.86	2.70	0.72	2.66
Indonesia	0.96	3.63	1.71	0.47	2.42
Iran	1.00	1.97	1.46	0.11	1.40
Japan	−0.42	1.46	0.38	0.24	0.42
Kazakhstan	0.33	3.85	3.05	0.28	0.85
Malaysia	1.62	3.63	2.37	0.47	2.42
Mexico	1.03	2.83	1.56	0.01	2.28
Pakistan	1.42	3.63	2.17	0.47	2.42
Russia	−0.53	4.17	2.53	0.36	0.76
Saudi Arabia	1.39	1.97	1.86	0.11	1.40
South Africa	−0.12	2.15	0.39	0.33	1.32
South Korea	0.15	3.61	2.89	0.56	0.31
Taiwan	0.11	3.63	0.86	0.47	2.42
Thailand	0.48	3.63	1.23	0.47	2.42
Turkey	1.09	2.00	2.42	0.41	0.26
Ukraine	−0.65	3.85	2.07	0.28	0.85
United States	0.96	1.78	2.20	0.23	0.31
Venezuela	1.39	2.36	3.17	0.35	0.23
25 emitters	0.77	2.87	1.96	0.29	1.39
Rest of world industrial	1.05	1.41	1.72	0.33	0.40
Rest of world developing	1.77	3.00	2.46	−0.40	2.70
World	1.05	2.76	2.08	0.24	1.49
Industrial	0.26	2.10	1.64	0.32	0.40
Developing	1.20	3.88	2.52	0.26	2.30

n = population; g = ppp GDP per capita; w = energy efficiency; c = carbon efficiency

Source: Author's calculations.

Table 2.4 Decomposition of emissions growth, 2020–30
(annual percent)

Country/economy	n	g	w	c	Emissions
Argentina	0.73	2.19	2.02	0.07	0.84
Australia	0.85	2.28	2.26	0.11	0.76
Brazil	0.76	2.84	1.43	−0.12	2.28
Canada	0.58	1.70	1.24	0.24	0.80
China	0.21	4.25	2.18	0.09	2.20
Egypt	1.43	1.29	1.40	0.04	1.29
European Union	−0.11	1.93	1.39	0.28	0.15
India	0.97	3.41	2.51	0.16	1.71
Indonesia	0.76	3.27	1.38	−0.23	2.88
Iran	0.59	2.01	1.01	−0.04	1.62
Japan	−0.69	0.86	0.35	0.35	−0.52
Kazakhstan	0.00	2.90	2.38	0.06	0.46
Malaysia	1.39	3.27	2.00	−0.23	2.88
Mexico	0.81	2.80	1.85	−0.02	1.78
Pakistan	1.25	3.27	1.87	−0.23	2.88
Russia	−0.64	3.01	1.92	0.29	0.17
Saudi Arabia	1.28	2.01	1.71	−0.04	1.62
South Africa	0.07	1.29	0.04	0.04	1.29
South Korea	−0.07	2.83	1.80	−0.02	0.97
Taiwan	−0.13	3.27	0.49	−0.23	2.88
Thailand	0.25	3.27	0.86	−0.23	2.88
Turkey	0.77	1.93	2.27	0.28	0.15
Ukraine	−0.75	2.90	1.63	0.06	0.46
United States	0.90	1.70	1.85	0.05	0.70
Venezuela	1.11	2.19	2.41	0.07	0.84
25 emitters	0.54	2.48	1.68	0.03	1.31
Rest of world industrial	0.67	1.55	1.59	0.14	0.48
Rest of world developing	1.56	3.00	2.76	−0.62	2.41
World	0.84	2.46	1.92	−0.03	1.41
Industrial	0.15	1.93	1.52	0.18	0.38
Developing	0.97	3.19	2.19	−0.08	2.05

n = population; g = ppp GDP per capita; w = energy efficiency; c = carbon efficiency

Source: Author's calculations.

ting countries, population growth decelerates from 1.1 percent annually in 1990–2006 to 0.77 percent in 2010–20 and 0.54 percent in 2020–30. Per capita growth accelerates, from 2.1 to 2.9 percent followed by 2.5 percent. Although the individual-country rates of growth per capita tend to remain stable or ease, the rising shares of China, India, and other rapidly growing emerging-market economies in global output boosts the overall per capita growth rate of the 25 major emitting countries. Annual growth in output efficiency of energy also rises, from 1.4 to 2.0 percent followed by 1.7 percent. Carbon efficiency (energy per unit of carbon) rises modestly and then ebbs again (from –0.03 to 0.29 percent, followed by 0.03 percent). In other words, the outlook is business as usual in two senses of the phrase: no special change from climate action and relative continuity (inertia) in the various factors contributing to emissions growth. Virtually the entire reduction in emissions growth from the recent historical period to the decade of the 2020s is accounted for by a half-percent deceleration in annual population growth. Although there is some acceleration in energy efficiency growth, it is offset by a rise in per capita GDP growth.

Extending the Baseline through 2050

Climate policy deliberations have focused on the period through 2050. Before examining abatement costs, it is therefore necessary to extend the bau baseline through 2050. Population projections by the US Census Bureau (2009) provide a basis for estimating the rate of growth of population (n) for 2030–40 and 2040–50. For economic growth per capita, energy efficiency growth, and carbon efficiency growth, the strong inertia just discussed suggests that a reasonable first approximation is continuation at the rates expected for the 2030s. Table 2.5 reports the resulting emissions growth components for 2030–40 and 2040–50, along with the resulting absolute levels of bau baseline emissions by 2040 and 2050. The emissions growth rates are simply the population growth rates for the decade in question plus continuation of the other growth rate components ($+g$, $-w$, $-c$) experienced in 2020–30 as shown in table 2.4.

The global level of CO_2 emissions by 2050 resulting from these assumptions turns out to be broadly compatible with the more plausible among the emissions paths considered in the 2007 IPCC report. Thus, in the second highest path in that assessment, "A2," global emissions were projected to reach 16.5 billion tons of carbon (GtC) by 2050, or 60.6 $GtCO_2$ (IPCC 2007a, 803), broadly similar to the estimate of 53.2 $GtCO_2$ in table 2.5.

Some recent studies have suggested that faster-than-expected emissions growth in the period 2000–06 means that the A2 path considerably understates likely future emissions, even though it had previously been regarded as being toward the higher end of reasonable scenarios (see, e.g., Sheehan 2008).[4]

---

4. Actual CO_2 emissions growth from 2000 to 2006 averaged 3.1 percent (van Vuuren and Riahi 2008, 241). In comparison, the highest of six scenarios considered by the IPCC (A1B) called for 3.4 percent annual growth from 2000 to 2010; the median scenario rate was 2.0 percent. Scenario

Table 2.5 Business as usual baseline, 2030–50

Country/economy	Population Annual growth (percent) 2030–40	2040–50	Emissions Annual growth (percent) 2030–40	2040–50	Levels (million tCO$_2$) 2040	2050
Argentina	0.55	0.37	0.66	0.48	241	252
Australia	0.61	0.46	0.53	0.38	457	474
Brazil	0.53	0.29	2.05	1.81	789	945
Canada	0.38	0.26	0.60	0.48	691	725
China	−0.05	−0.21	1.93	1.77	14,426	17,220
Egypt	1.20	0.96	1.06	0.82	266	288
European Union	−0.24	−0.37	0.02	−0.10	4,143	4,101
India	0.73	0.53	1.47	1.27	2,863	3,249
Indonesia	0.54	0.27	2.66	2.39	826	1,049
Iran	0.27	0.11	1.30	1.14	832	932
Japan	−0.89	−1.03	−0.72	−0.86	1,116	1,023
Kazakhstan	−0.19	−0.37	0.27	0.09	242	245
Malaysia	1.11	0.91	2.60	2.40	463	588
Mexico	0.56	0.34	1.54	1.31	657	749
Pakistan	1.01	0.76	2.64	2.39	353	448
Russia	−0.63	−0.65	0.18	0.15	1,847	1,876
Saudi Arabia	1.42	1.24	1.76	1.58	711	833
South Africa	0.04	0.07	1.26	1.29	675	767
South Korea	−0.44	−0.79	0.61	0.26	666	684
Taiwan	−0.49	−0.82	2.52	2.19	666	829
Thailand	−0.00	−0.22	2.63	2.41	673	856
Turkey	0.51	0.24	−0.12	−0.38	272	261
Ukraine	−0.78	−0.84	0.43	0.37	406	422
United States	0.83	0.79	0.62	0.59	6,644	7,046
Venezuela	0.82	0.59	0.54	0.32	235	242
25 emitters	0.35	0.20	1.21	1.14	41,159	46,107
Rest of world industrial	0.32	0.04	0.13	−0.15	548	540
Rest of world developing	1.35	1.17	2.14	1.90	5,416	6,549
World	0.67	0.53	1.30	1.21	47,123	53,196
Industrial	0.07	0.01	0.28	0.22	15,446	15,785
Developing	0.77	0.61	1.83	1.66	31,677	37,410

Source: Author's calculations.

However, global economic growth was unusually rapid in this period, averaging 5 percent annually in 2004–07 versus 3.4 percent in 2000–03 and 3 percent in 1990–99 (ppp GDP; IMF 2010). In contrast, the global financial crisis cut world economic growth to an average of only 1.1 percent per year in 2008–09. Correspondingly, there was an estimated 1.3 percent decline in global emissions from 2008 to 2009 (Myhre, Alterskjaer, and Lowe 2010). Even before the global recession some analysts judged that the recent emissions trends overstated prospective long-term growth and that there was no reason yet to depart from the range of emissions scenarios previously considered by the IPCC (van Vuuren and Riahi 2008). Nonetheless, to the extent that the bau baseline used here is understated, the estimates of emissions reductions and abatement costs will also tend to be understated.

The carbon dioxide emissions baseline includes only emissions from fossil fuels and industrial processes. Although emissions from deforestation and land use are also currently important, at about 4 $GtCO_2$ per year, the IPCC emissions scenarios typically anticipate that they will decline substantially, falling to a median of 1.1 $GtCO_2$ by 2030 and 0.6 $GtCO_2$ by 2050 (IPCC 2001, 801).[5] These levels are sufficiently low to omit from the analysis, especially considering that although their inclusion would tend to boost the baseline (modestly), it would also tend to reduce unit abatement costs (because of low-cost opportunities in afforestation and reduced deforestation). Finally, non-CO_2 greenhouse gases and aerosols are also omitted from the main analysis. Appendix C considers their additional influence and estimates that a target of 450 ppm for CO_2-equivalent including other greenhouse gases and aerosols would translate to a more ambitious target of 414 ppm for carbon dioxide itself.

A2 was at the median through 2010 but second highest by 2050, with average annual growth for 2000–50 amounting to 1.7 percent (versus 2.4 percent in the highest path, A1T). Calculated from IPCC (2001, 801).

5. However, in scenario A2 deforestation and land use still account for about 4 $GtCO_2$ by 2030 and about 3 $GtCO_2$ by 2050.

3

Abatement Initiatives in the Copenhagen Accord and Cancún Agreements

In December 2009, heads of state met in Copenhagen for the 15th Conference of Parties of the United Nations Framework Convention on Climate Change (UNFCCC). In the resulting Copenhagen Accord they pledged targets for emissions reductions by 2020. For the first time, major emerging-market and developing countries undertook abatement pledges. Their previous omission had been a serious shortcoming of the Kyoto Protocol. Subsequently incorporated more formally into the UNFCCC at the 16th Conference of Parties in November–December 2010 in Cancún, Mexico, the Copenhagen Accord pledges provide the best basis for identifying prospective abatement paths through 2020. Together with policy scenarios developed in this study for subsequent international action, they serve as the basis for the abatement cost estimates compiled in chapters 5 and 6.

As set forth in chapter 5, the 2020 targets are only a modest beginning in the task of limiting global warming. They would reduce global emissions from about 35.9 billion tons of carbon dioxide ($GtCO_2$) under business as usual (bau) to 32.7 $GtCO_2$ (table 5.1 in chapter 5), a cutback of only 9 percent. Reductions would be 17 percent from 2005 levels for the United States and 20 percent below 1990 levels for the European Union. Because bau emissions paths are virtually flat through 2020 for these two leading world economies, the corresponding cutbacks from baseline are both approximately 17 percent as well (tables 2.2 and 5.3). Among emerging-market economies, Brazil, Indonesia, Mexico, South Korea, and South Africa pledged cutbacks of approximately one-third from the 2020 baselines. In contrast, China and India pledged cutbacks in carbon intensity of GDP (by 40 to 45 percent and 20 to 25 percent from 2005 levels, respectively). However, because of anticipated increases in energy efficiency even in the bau baseline, the resulting emissions levels for these two largest emerging-market nations would not require cutbacks from baseline. Even so, the limits would constrain any tendency toward "carbon leakage" through increased carbon-based export activity that could result from complete free-riding.

Copenhagen Accord Pledges

The Copenhagen Accord (see UNFCCC 2010a) called for limiting warming to 2°C and stated that an assessment by 2015 should determine whether the goal should be further strengthened to a limit of 1.5°C. Under the Accord, Annex I parties of the UNFCCC (industrial and former transition economies) were expected to submit "economy-wide emissions targets" for 2020. Other (emerging-market and developing) economies were invited to submit voluntary "nationally appropriate mitigation actions." Table 3.1 lists the pledges of the main emitting economies.

The United States set as its 2020 target a reduction of emissions by 17 percent from the level in 2005 as the base year (5.8 $GtCO_2$; CDIAC 2009). It also stated a reduction of 83 percent below the 2005 level as the target for 2050. These were also the targets in the Waxman-Markey bill passed by the House of Representatives in June 2009 (Govtrack 2009). The European Union pledged to reduce emissions by 20 percent by 2020 from 1990 levels and by as much as 30 percent "provided that other developed countries commit themselves to comparable emission reductions and that developing countries contribute adequately to their responsibilities and respective capabilities" (UNFCCC 2010a). The most likely prospect, however, is that the European Union will not consider other efforts sufficient and hence will remain with the 20 percent cut target for 2020. In its submission, the European Union further stated that developed countries should reduce emissions by 80 to 95 percent below 1990 levels by 2050, so implicitly the EU target for itself by 2050 is at least an 80 percent cut.

Among other major industrial economies, Japan pledged a 25 percent reduction by 2020 from its 1990 base, "premised on the establishment of a fair and effective international framework in which all major economies participate and on agreement by those economies on ambitious targets." Canada pledged a cut of 17 percent by 2020 from a base year of 2005, "to be aligned with the final economy-wide emissions target of the United States in enacted legislation." Australia pledged unconditionally a 5 percent cut by 2020 below 2000 levels. It also pledged a cut of up to 25 percent if an ambitious international agreement were reached that would stabilize CO_2-equivalent concentrations at 450 parts per million (ppm); and of up to 15 percent for a less ambitious agreement in which "major developing economies commit to substantially restrain emissions and advanced economies take on commitments comparable to Australia's." (The calculations below place Australia's cut at 10 percent.)

The major emerging-market economies chose two alternative approaches for their pledges of nationally appropriate mitigation measures. Brazil, Indonesia, Mexico, South Korea, and South Africa undertook cuts of about one-

Table 3.1   Country targets and initiatives under the Copenhagen Accord

Country	Pledge for emissions reduction by 2020	Base year	2007 level[a] (million tons of CO_2)
Annex I			
Australia	5 percent (15 or 25 percent contingent)	2000	377
Canada	Same as the United States	2005	530
European Union	20 percent (30 percent contingent); implied 80 percent by 2050	1990	4,050
Japan	25 percent (contingent)	1990	1,236
New Zealand	10 to 20 percent (contingent)	1990	39
Norway	30 to 40 percent	1990	46
Russia	15 to 25 percent	1990	1,585
Switzerland	20 percent (30 percent contingent)	1990	46
United States	17 percent; 83 percent by 2050	2005	5,812
Other			
Argentina	Measures for energy efficiency and support to renewable energy	—	172
Brazil	36 to 39 percent cut by 2020; focus on deforestation and agriculture	bau	352
China	40 to 45 percent cut in carbon intensity of GDP; 15 percent nonfossil energy	2005	6,603
India	20 to 25 percent cut in carbon intensity of GDP	2005	1,574
Indonesia	26 percent; focus on afforestation, reduced deforestation	bau	416
Kazakhstan	15 percent	1992	195
Mexico	30 percent	bau	445
Singapore	16 percent	bau	148
South Africa	34 percent	bau	434
South Korea	30 percent	bau	477
Total			24,537

bau = business as usual

a. Excludes deforestation.

Source: Table 2.2; US Energy Information Administration; and UNFCCC, Copenhagen Accord, http://unfccc.int/home/items/5262.php.

third from bau baselines otherwise attained by 2020. In the case of Brazil, about two-thirds of the overall cut of 36 to 39 percent was to come from forestry and agricultural measures. Considering that deforestation accounts for about half of Brazil's emissions, the implication is that industrial emissions (the emissions considered in the analysis of this study) would be cut from the bau baseline by about 24 percent.[1]

China and India chose the other main alternative of the major emerging-market economies: statement of a target expressed as a reduction in the carbon intensity of GDP. China pledged a reduction of 40 to 45 percent in carbon dioxide emissions per unit of economic output by 2020 compared with the 2005 base. It also pledged to increase the share of non-fossil fuels in primary energy consumption to 15 percent by 2020 and set specific targets for increased forest coverage. Its submission specifically referred to UNFCCC Article 4, paragraph 7, which premises developing-country action on industrial-country implementation of commitments on financial resources and transfer of technology. For its part, India set as its goal a reduction in the nonagricultural emissions intensity of GDP by 20 to 25 percent by 2020 from the 2005 level. India also cited Article 4, paragraph 7.

The bau projections set forth above provide a basis for examining the meaning of the pledges by China and India. China's CO_2 emissions stood at 5.63 billion tons in 2005 (CDIAC 2009). Its bau baseline is at 9.54 $GtCO_2$ by 2020 (table 2.2). The baseline emissions multiple from 2005 to 2020 is thus 1.69. In comparison, for 2005–20 per capita GDP growth is expected to average 6.9 percent per year (appendix table A.2) and population growth 0.6 percent, placing total growth at 7.5 percent per year. This growth would increase GDP by a multiple of 2.96. Shrinking the ratio of emissions to GDP by 42.5 percent would translate to an expansion of emissions from 2005 to 2020 by a multiple of 1.70.[2] So the pledged reduction in carbon intensity is almost identical to the expected bau baseline. For purposes of the calculations in this study, it is assumed that China has zero departure from baseline by 2020 in the central policy scenario (Copenhagen Convergence) based on the Copenhagen Accord.[3]

The same calculation for India shows the following. Baseline emissions rise by a multiple of 1.46, from 1.42 $GtCO_2$ in 2005 (CDIAC 2009) to 2.08 $GtCO_2$ in 2020 (table 2.2). Real GDP grows at 6.3 percent through 2020 (5 percent per capita plus 1.3 percent population growth), yielding an expansion multiple of 2.50 from 2005 to 2020. Shrinking the GDP expansion by the goal for reduced

---

1. That is, of a total cut of 36 percent from bau, two-thirds or 24 percent would be in forestry and agriculture, implying a cut from baseline of 48 percent in these sectors. The remaining 12 percent of the total would amount to 24 percent of the half of total emissions coming from the industrial sector.

2. That is, 2.96×0.575.

3. China's Energy Research Institute of the National Development and Reform Commission (NDRC) issued projections in 2009 that are extremely close to those used here (ERI 2009). The ERI places baseline emissions in 2020 (in the absence of a commitment to reducing carbon dioxide emissions) at 10.2 $GtCO_2$ (p. 806). Given the report's projections of economic and population growth, the implied carbon intensity of GDP declines by 42.4 percent. The corresponding estimates here are 9.5 $GtCO_2$ and 42.9 percent.

carbon intensity yields a permitted expansion of emissions by a multiple of 1.94.[4] So for India also, the target is not a constraint on bau emissions. Indeed, in the case of India the pledge includes a sizable cushion of about 33 percent.[5] India is also treated in the relevant calculations below as having a zero cut from bau baseline by 2020 in the Copenhagen Convergence scenario.

The diagnosis that the Chinese and Indian offers at Copenhagen would not constrain them from their bau baselines can be examined from another perspective: How do their promised rates of increase in carbon efficiency of output compare with those over a comparable period in the past? From 1990 to 2006, emissions rose at annual growth rates of 5.8 percent for China and 4.9 percent for India (table 2.1). Real GDP rose at 9.7 percent for China and 6.1 percent for India (table 2.1, sum of n and g). So carbon efficiency of output ($w + c$, as distinguished from carbon efficiency of energy, c) rose at the difference, or 3.9 percent per year in China and 1.2 percent per year in India.[6] Over the span of 15 years, these rates translate to a reduction in carbon per unit of output by 43.5 and 16.1 percent, respectively. So it turns out that at Copenhagen, China promised to do just as well as it has done over the past 15 years, but not better. India promised to do a bit better than it has in the past, reducing carbon requirements of output by about 22 percent rather than about 16 percent. It can be argued, nonetheless, that for China to continue its high rate of reduction of carbon per unit of output would be an important accomplishment. As shown in table 2.1, for the 25 largest emitting nations (with the EU treated as one) the average rate of growth in carbon efficiency of output was 1.33 percent per year in 1990–2006 ($w + c$ in the table). China's corresponding rate was 3.89 percent, almost three times as high despite coming solely from rising energy efficiency that far exceeded falling carbon efficiency.

It should be recognized that what amounts to a bau pledge through 2020 from China and India represents a contribution to global abatement in at least one further sense. In the absence of such undertakings, emissions from China and India might rise well above the bau baseline as a consequence of "carbon leakage" through production and trade responses to new opportunities presented as other nations cut back carbon-intensive production.

Cancún Agreements

The 16th Conference of Parties of the UNFCCC in Cancún in effect legitimated within the United Nations framework the politically crucial but more ad hoc pledges offered by major countries a year before at Copenhagen, where obstruction by six countries had forced the UNFCCC merely to "take note"

---

4. That is, 2.50×0.775.

5. That is, $1.94/1.46$.

6. Carbon efficiency of output rises at the sum of carbon efficiency of energy, c, and energy efficiency of output, w.

of rather than adopt the Copenhagen Accord.[7] This time a forceful chairman, Mexican Foreign Minister Patricia Espinosa, declared that "consensus does not mean unanimity" and 193 Parties to the UNFCCC adopted the Cancún Agreements despite the opposition of a single country, Bolivia (Stavins 2010).

Beyond endorsing the Copenhagen pledges, the Cancún agreements provided for a mechanism to monitor the progress of countries in meeting the commitments; established the Cancún Adaptation Framework for assistance to vulnerable countries in adjusting to climate change already under way (including a new climate fund managed by the World Bank); and spelled out steps for national action plans for curbing deforestation. For the first time in an official United Nations accord the agreements also adopted the objective of limiting global warming to no more than 2°C above preindustrial levels (UNFCCC 2010b, Houser 2010b, Stavins 2010).

The European Union and some other parties (including Japan, Australia, Russia, and Canada) seek to transform the Cancún Agreements and the mitigation pledges of the Copenhagen Accord into a legally binding international treaty as the successor to the Kyoto Protocol, which expires in 2012. It seems far more likely, however, that progress will have to occur on the more informal basis implied by the very name of the Ad Hoc Working Group set up at Copenhagen. In the pivotal case of the United States, climate legislation stalled after passage of the Waxman-Markey bill in 2009, as the Great Recession shifted priorities and landmark health care legislation as well as financial regulatory reform preempted attention. For some time it may fall to the Environmental Protection Agency as well as three state-level regional initiatives to implement what amounts to a Plan B for mitigation (Cline 2010b).

For the purposes of the present study, the principal implication of the Cancún Agreements is that they strengthen the international political commitment (albeit not in a legally binding fashion) to the abatement targets that emerged in the Copenhagen Accord and that are the basis for the estimates for abatement costs and emissions levels by 2020.

---

7. UNFCCC (2010a, Decision 2/CP.15). The formal name for the Copenhagen undertakings, subsequently used frequently in the Cancún Agreements (UNFCCC 2010b), is Ad Hoc Working Group on Long-term Cooperative Action Under the Convention. At Copenhagen the dissenting countries were Bolivia, Cuba, Nicaragua, Sudan, Tuvalu, and Venezuela. For an account of the negotiations at Copenhagen, see Houser (2010a).

4

Abatement Cost Functions

This chapter sets forth the next building block in the analysis of this study: equations and parameters for estimating abatement cost as a function of the depth of emissions cut from baseline. Three sets of estimates are used in this study. Two are from the "top down" school, in which overall economic output is cut back in a nonlinear fashion as emissions are reduced. The widely used "RICE" model of William Nordhaus (2010b) has a nearly cubic cost function. In a second set of top-down estimates the survey of other leading models in the Stanford Energy Modeling Forum (EMF) provides the basis for new estimates of region-specific abatement cost curves developed in the present study (appendix G). The third set of estimates is from the "bottom up" analysis of McKinsey (2009), in which the focus is on a sequence of successively more costly operations to cut emissions (with initial activities such as a shift to fluorescent lighting having negative cost if institutional obstacles can be overcome).

The broad effect is that the cheapest abatement is found in the McKinsey curves; next is the RICE abatement cost, which can be very low in initial cutbacks but mounts rapidly; and highest are the EMF 22 costs, which begin much higher but rise less rapidly with less-than-quadratic parameters. With the quantitative estimates of the cost functions obtained in this chapter, it is possible to apply the abatement policy scenarios examined in the next chapter to arrive at estimates of prospective costs of international action to limit climate change.

Top-Down and Bottom-Up Models

There are two schools of carbon abatement cost curves. The first is the "bottom up" school based on specific operations (e.g., shifting to fluorescent lighting in buildings, at the low-cost end, or car hybridization, at the high-cost end). This school typically identifies some initial portion of emissions that can be eliminated at zero or even negative cost, representing existing inefficiencies in energy use. Such market imperfections as lack of finance for investment in energy-saving measures with multi-year recovery periods, and "agency" problems (for example, an apartment dweller does not reap the long-term benefits of energy-efficiency investments), are invoked as causes of such opportunities for "free" emissions savings. The second is the "top down" school, which typically models abatement costs at the aggregate economywide level as a nonlinear function of the extent of the target carbon cutback from the business as usual (bau) baseline. Creyts et al. (2007) provide an example of the influential McKinsey estimates in the bottom-up tradition; Nordhaus (2008, 2010b) represents a leading top-down model. Both schools tend to identify reductions in abatement costs over time, for a given target percent cutback from bau emissions, as a consequence of a widening menu of technological alternatives. One of the most important of these is carbon capture and sequestration as a potential means of future burning of coal with minimal emissions, a technology whose feasibility so far remains to be demonstrated on substantial scale. The estimates developed in the present study turn out to show a range from low abatement costs based on the McKinsey bottom-up model to intermediate in the Nordhaus top-down model to relatively high costs using equations estimated from the EMF 22 survey of integrated assessment models (see appendix G).

RICE Model

The form used by Nordhaus (2008) for calculating abatement cost, and also applied in the new EMF-based estimates developed in the present study, is as follows:

$$k_t = \alpha_t \mu_t^{\beta} \tag{4.1}$$

where k is abatement cost as a fraction of GDP, α is a parameter that declines over time to reflect the widening menu of technological alternatives, μ is the "control rate" or proportionate reduction in emissions from the bau baseline to the policy target level, β is the exponent showing the degree of nonlinearity in costs for deeper cuts, and as before t is the year in question. In his regional RICE model, Nordhaus sets the degree of nonlinearity uniformly at $\beta = 2.8$, or nearly cubic, for all countries and time periods. Table 4.1 reports his time- and country-varying cost parameter α for the 25 major emitting economies examined in this study.[1] For example, in order to cut US emissions by 40 percent from baseline by 2030, it would require an opportunity cost to the economy of

---

1. Values are from the online version of the RICE model available at http://nordhaus.econ.yale.edu/RICEmodels.htm. Note that Nordhaus uses θ_1 and θ_2 for the terms α and β here. The model provides specific estimates for the following economies: United States, European Union, Japan, Russia, China, and India. All other estimates shown here are from the relevant regional groupings in the model: Africa, Latin America, Middle East, Eurasia, Other Asia, and Other High Income.

Table 4.1 Multiplicative abatement cost parameter (α) in the Nordhaus RICE model

Country/region	2020	2030	2040	2050
United States	0.036	0.029	0.024	0.020
European Union	0.034	0.028	0.024	0.021
Japan	0.047	0.039	0.032	0.027
Russia	0.044	0.036	0.030	0.025
Eurasia	0.049	0.038	0.030	0.024
China	0.063	0.049	0.038	0.030
India	0.066	0.052	0.042	0.034
Middle East	0.055	0.045	0.037	0.031
Africa	0.042	0.033	0.026	0.021
Latin America	0.038	0.032	0.027	0.023
Other high income	0.048	0.039	0.032	0.027
Other non-OECD Asia	0.070	0.057	0.046	0.039

OECD = Organization for Economic Cooperation and Development

Source: Nordhaus (2010b).

$k = 0.029 \times 0.40^{2.8} = 0.0022$, or 0.22 percent of GDP. As indicated in the table, for a given percent cut from baseline, by 2050 the cost is only about half as large (as a percent of GDP) as it would be in 2020. The declining cost, combined with a relatively high long-term discount rate, contributes to the "ramp-up" profile (relatively moderate initial cuts followed by rising proportional cuts) of the optimal abatement paths found in studies by Nordhaus (2008, 2010a).

The 2010 version of the RICE model (Nordhaus 2010b), from which table 4.1 is taken, derives the abatement cost parameters from models with national and regional detail in the Fourth Assessment Report (IPCC 2007b) and the Energy Modeling Forum (EMF) 22 report (Clarke, Böhringer, and Rutherford 2009), as indicated in Nordhaus (2010a, 6).

EMF 22 Models

Appendix G applies the same functional form of equation 4.1 to estimate cost functions from the large set of model results compiled in EMF 22. It turns out that the estimated equations show a strong pattern of higher abatement costs than those of the RICE model for moderate emissions cutbacks but more comparable estimates for large cutbacks. Correspondingly, the equations estimated in appendix G show much less nonlinearity than indicated by the RICE parameters, with the exponent on the proportionate cutback always less than quadratic rather than nearly cubic.

Table 4.2 reports the EMF-based estimates of the multiplicative cost coefficient α (equation 4.1) as well as the exponential coefficient (β), which varies

Table 4.2 Abatement cost function parameters, EMF 22 synthesis model

Country/group	2020	2030	2040	2050
A. Multiplicative (a)				
China	0.087	0.087	0.100	0.078
European Union	0.025	0.025	0.024	0.024
India	0.090	0.090	0.066	0.066
United States	0.049	0.049	0.023	0.023
Group 1	0.031	0.031	0.030	0.021
Group 2	0.101	0.101	0.073	0.073
Group 3	0.092	0.092	0.102	0.070
B. Exponential (β)				
China	1.381	1.381	1.586	1.586
European Union	1.278	1.278	1.442	1.442
India	1.545	1.545	1.412	1.412
United States	1.569	1.569	1.158	1.158
Group 1	1.457	1.457	1.612	1.612
Group 2	1.532	1.532	1.336	1.336
Group 3	1.413	1.413	1.764	1.764

Group 1: Other Annex I countries excluding Russia (i.e., developed countries).
Group 2: BRICs (Brazil, Russia, India, and China).
Group 3: Other countries (i.e., developing countries other than the BRICs).

Source: Appendix G.

by region and time period rather than being universally a single value (2.8 in the RICE model). Figure 4.1 illustrates results comparing the RICE cost function with the EMF-based estimate for selected regions (the United States, the European Union, China, and Latin America) under standardized cuts from baseline (20 percent in 2020, 40 percent in 2030, 60 percent in 2040, and 80 percent in 2050). In all cases the EMF-based equations show higher cost than the RICE equations. For example, for the United States, a cutback of 40 percent from baseline in 2030 would cost 1.15 percent of GDP in the EMF-based estimates but only 0.22 percent of GDP in the RICE-based estimates. The divergence is the greatest for developing countries. Thus, again for a 40 percent cut in 2030, the EMF-based cost would be about 2½ percent of GDP for China and for Latin America, whereas the RICE-based cost would be only 0.36 percent of GDP for China and 0.25 percent for Latin America.[2]

---

2. The EMF-based equations are specific to the region for China but for Latin America are from the EMF general category "Group 3" of developing countries other than the BRICs (Brazil, Russia, India, and China).

Figure 4.1   Comparison of RICE and EMF 22–based abatement cost estimates for uniform cuts from baseline[a]

percent of GDP

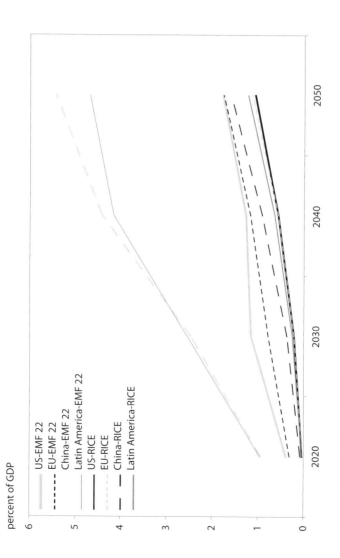

a. Cuts from baseline: 20 percent in 2020, 40 percent in 2030, 60 percent in 2040, 80 percent in 2050.

Source: Author's calculations, based on tables 4.1 and 4.2.

McKinsey Model

For the bottom-up school, the most prominent abatement cost estimates are those of McKinsey (2009). Ackerman, Stanton, and Bueno (2010) have obtained detailed regional estimates from the McKinsey study and developed summary equations approximating cost curves for 2030 by region. These curves are of the form:

$$z' = A \frac{R}{B-R} \tag{4.2}$$

where z' is marginal cost per unit of carbon dioxide reduction, R is the amount of the reduction, B is the quantity of reduction at which the marginal cost curve turns vertical (infinite cost for an additional unit of abatement), and A is a cost parameter. The CRED model of Ackerman, Stanton, and Bueno (2010) estimates this equation for nine regions, based on the McKinsey estimates.[3] Importantly, the equation form chosen by Ackerman et al. does not allow for the well-known initial negative marginal cost in the McKinsey estimates but instead treats costs in the initial range as close to zero but not negative.

To obtain an estimate of total cost of abatement, it is necessary to integrate the marginal cost function over the span from zero to the cutback of R. This integral is:

$$z = \int_0^R z' = A[B \ln \frac{B}{B-R} - R] \tag{4.3}$$

Table 4.3 reports these bottom-up abatement parameters for 2030, in billions of dollars at 2005 prices (parameter A) and billion tons of carbon (B).[4] For example, for the United States in 2030 the reduction at which marginal cost turns infinite is 1.39 GtC, or 5.1 $GtCO_2$. Considering that the baseline emissions for 2030 stand at 6.24 $GtCO_2$ (table 2.2), marginal cost turns infinite at 82 percent cutback from baseline. For most countries the estimates in table 4.3 apply 2030 baseline shares in total emissions for the relevant region to obtain the B scaled to the country in question.[5]

---

3. The nine regions are United States, Europe, Other High Income, Latin America, Middle East, Russia and non-EU Eastern Europe, Africa, China, and South and Southeast Asia.

4. For industrial emissions only.

5. There is no attempt to estimate the parameters for Rest of World Developing, because in the calculations later this grouping never carries out abatement because its per capita emissions are always lower than the 2050 global convergence level. See appendix table A.3.

Table 4.3   Ackerman et al. abatement cost parameters from McKinsey for 2030

Country	Parameter A (billions of 2005 dollars)	Parameter B (GtC)
Argentina	51.53	0.04
Australia	107.41	0.09
Brazil	51.53	0.08
Canada	107.41	0.13
China	66.39	2.64
Egypt	64.5	0.04
European Union	101.91	0.76
India	53.9	0.52
Indonesia	53.9	0.12
Iran	46.53	0.12
Japan	107.41	0.30
Kazakhstan	36.8	0.05
Malaysia	53.9	0.07
Mexico	51.53	0.10
Pakistan	53.9	0.05
Russia	36.8	0.38
Saudi Arabia	46.53	0.10
South Africa	64.5	0.11
South Korea	53.9	0.16
Taiwan	53.9	0.09
Thailand	53.9	0.09
Turkey	101.91	0.05
Ukraine	36.8	0.08
United States	64.74	1.39
Venezuela	51.53	0.04
Rest of world industrial	107.41	0.12

Source: Calculated from Ackerman et al. (2010).

5

Abatement Costs through 2050

In the central Copenhagen Convergence (CopCon) international policy scenario of this chapter, countries adhere to their Copenhagen targets by 2020. Thereafter they follow a linear path of emissions reductions such that by 2050 there is uniformity in per capita emissions in all countries, at 1.43 tons of CO_2 per person per year. This amount is consistent with remaining within the 2°C limit on global warming incorporated in the Copenhagen Accord. The equity-based principle of equalization in per capita emissions is premised on the need to mobilize cooperation from key emerging-market economies that otherwise might refuse to limit emissions on grounds that their per capita levels are much lower than those of rich countries. By 2050 cutbacks from the business as usual (bau) baseline reach about 90 percent for the United States, Australia, and Canada, and 84 percent for the European Union. More surprisingly, cutbacks from baseline also reach 85 to 90 percent for numerous emerging-market economies, including China, Malaysia, Russia, Saudi Arabia, South Africa, and South Korea. Rapid baseline economic growth means proportionate 2050 cuts comparable to those in industrial countries.

To accomplish these cutbacks, for 2020–50 the combined efficiency growth in output relative to energy and energy relative to carbon would need to rise from the baseline 2 percent annually to 6 percent annually. Most of the increase would likely need to come from a shift away from carbon-based energy. Global emissions would fall 9 percent from baseline by 2020, 35 percent by 2030, 57 percent by 2040, and 75 percent by 2050.

In the RICE cost functions, global abatement costs would be only 0.22 percent of world product by 2030, reaching 1.2 percent by 2050. In 2050 the cost would be 1.6 percent of product for industrial countries and 1.0 percent for developing countries. The abatement costs are much lower for the McKinsey cost function but substantially higher for the Energy Modeling Forum 22 (EMF 22) based functions (1.3 percent of world product by 2030 and 2.9 percent by 2050). Other major studies have found comparable ranges (IPCC 2007b, CBO 2009, Nordhaus 2010a), but one study featuring macroeconomic and monetary interactions places the costs much higher (McKibben, Morris, and Wilcoxen 2010).

Alternative policy scenarios include those of the United Nations Development Program (UNDP 2007), Chakravarty et al. (2009), and Frankel (2008). For 2050 the UNDP cuts reach 80 percent from 1990 levels for industrial countries and 20 percent for developing countries. The result is a high dispersion in 2050 emissions per capita (for example, South Korea at 4.5 tons versus India at 0.33). The Chakravarty et al. approach applies cuts based on the number of middle- and higher-income persons in each country (but estimates do not extend through 2050). The Frankel approach applies principles combining political feasibility and ethical norms. Applying the RICE cost functions (appendix E), for industrial countries the UNDP costs are higher than under CopCon in the initial decades but lower by 2050. Abatement costs are lower in the Chakravarty et al. and Frankel paths, which call for less ambitious cuts. Atmospheric concentrations in 2050 fall from 494 parts per million (ppm) in the bau baseline to 437 ppm under CopCon, 429 ppm under the UNDP scenario, and 460 ppm in the Frankel path.

Copenhagen Convergence (CopCon)

The central policy scenario in the cost estimates below is premised on a Copenhagen Accord path from 2010 to 2020. Thereafter, it is assumed that all countries pursue a linear declining path of emissions that by 2050 reaches international convergence in emissions per capita at a level consistent with keeping atmospheric concentrations at 450 ppm or below and global warming at a central expected amount of 2°C. This target warming ceiling was specifically mentioned in the Copenhagen Accord (UNFCCC 2010a). A central estimate of 2°C translates to an atmospheric concentration of 450 ppm for CO_2-equivalent (CO_2-e) (IPCC 2007a, 66). The relationships developed in appendix C indicate that after taking account of the warming effect of other greenhouse gases and the cooling effect of aerosols, the corresponding concentration for carbon dioxide alone would be 414 ppm.

In the most recent Intergovernmental Panel on Climate Change (IPCC) report, the upper bound for emissions by 2050, for compatibility with stabilization of concentrations at 440 to 490 ppm CO_2-e, is 13.3 billion tons of CO_2 ($GtCO_2$) (alone, not equivalent) annually, following a path that would decline to 10 $GtCO_2$ by 2060 and about 4 $GtCO_2$ by 2080 (IPCC 2007b, figure SPM.11). This 2050 level would correspond to 1.43 $GtCO_2$ per capita globally. On this basis, the 2050 per capita global target applied in the CopCon scenario is 1.43 $GtCO_2$. Applying a summary formula developed in appendix B to cumulative emissions that would occur under the CopCon scenario, atmospheric carbon dioxide concentration would be held to 437 ppm by 2050. Applying the formula developed in appendix C, this level for carbon dioxide alone would correspond to 476 ppm for total CO_2-e including other greenhouse gases and aerosols.

For the United States, a cut to the global per capita average of 1.43 tCO_2 by 2050 would be more ambitious than the 83 percent cut from 2005 pledged at Copenhagen (which would yield 2.26 tCO_2 per capita). Similarly, the 80 percent cut from 1990 levels implicitly pledged by the European Union at Copenhagen would leave 2050 emissions per capita above the global uniform target of CopCon (at 1.83 tCO_2 instead of 1.43 tCO_2). The policy scenario here assumes that if the United States and other industrial countries are to be successful in mobilizing such nations as China and India to commit to deep emissions cuts, they will need to accept the notion that the right to emit carbon dioxide has an economic value (equal to the international trading price in carbon rights at the time in question) and that there is no ethical basis in the long run for distributing this benefit other than on an equal per capita basis.

Figure 5.1 shows bau baseline emissions (panel A) and CopCon abatement emissions paths (panel B) for the United States, China, all other industrial countries, and all other developing countries. Again, the analysis here treats Russia as an industrial country.

Table 5.1 reports the bau baseline and CopCon target emissions paths for the countries considered here for 2020 and 2050, as well as the ratio of the target level to the baseline level.

The depth of cut from baseline for 2020 turns out to be identical for the European Union and the United States, at 17 percent. The cuts from baseline are somewhat larger for Canada (23 percent), Australia (26 percent), and especially Japan (30 percent). Several major emerging-market economies (but not China or India) carry out cuts from baseline in the range of 25 to 35 percent (Brazil, Indonesia, Mexico, South Africa, and South Korea).

By 2050 the cuts from the bau baseline reach 91 to 92 percent for the United States, Australia, and Canada, among industrial countries, but also for Russia, Kazakhstan, and Saudi Arabia. In all cases the deep cuts reflect the unusually high per capita emissions at present and in the bau baseline (see table A.3 in appendix A), in contrast with the CopCon target of globally equal per capita emissions by 2050. It is somewhat more surprising that there are also cuts from baseline on the order of 85 to 90 percent by 2050 for a relatively long list of other developing countries not presently near the high end of per capita emissions. These include China, Iran, Malaysia, South Africa, South Korea, Thailand, and Ukraine. Essentially their rapid bau baseline growth (especially in the case of China) means that by 2050 they reach per capita emissions close to those of the current high-end emitting nations, in the absence of abatement measures.

It is useful to translate these emissions cuts into corresponding required accelerations in total efficiency of carbon use. As outlined above, achieving the abatement path may be seen as being accomplished by accelerating the

Figure 5.1 Business as usual and Copenhagen Convergence abatement emissions paths, 1990–2050

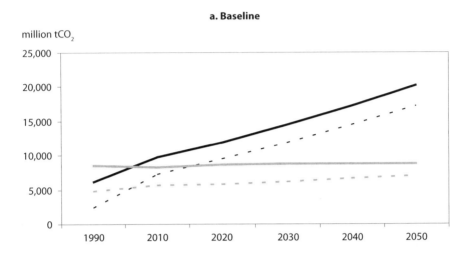

a. Baseline

million tCO$_2$

b. Abatement path

million tCO$_2$

- - - - - United States   - - - - - China
——— All other industrial countries   ——— All other developing countries

Source: Tables 2.2, 2.5, and D.1.

annual growth rate of energy efficiency of output combined with carbon efficiency of energy, or $w + c$. Table 5.2 reports the baseline and target path annual combined growth rates of energy efficiency of output and carbon efficiency of energy and shows the corresponding implied acceleration required.

Table 5.1   Business as usual (bau) baseline and Copenhagen Convergence (CopCon) target emissions, 2020 and 2050 (million tCO$_2$)

Country/group	bau baseline 2020	bau baseline 2050	CopCon abatement 2020	CopCon abatement 2050	Ratio 2020	Ratio 2050
Argentina	207	252	207	77	1.00	0.30
Australia	401	474	296	41	0.74	0.09
Brazil	511	945	389	373	0.76	0.39
Canada	601	725	465	59	0.77	0.08
China	9,544	17,220	9,544	2,037	1.00	0.12
Egypt	210	288	210	197	1.00	0.68
European Union	4,070	4,101	3,360	657	0.83	0.16
India	2,083	3,249	2,083	2,369	1.00	0.73
Indonesia	475	1,049	351	448	0.74	0.43
Iran	621	932	621	117	1.00	0.13
Japan	1,264	1,023	879	134	0.70	0.13
Kazakhstan	225	245	222	22	0.99	0.09
Malaysia	267	588	267	62	1.00	0.11
Mexico	471	749	330	212	0.70	0.28
Pakistan	203	448	203	395	1.00	0.88
Russia	1,785	1,876	1,660	156	0.93	0.08
Saudi Arabia	508	833	508	71	1.00	0.09
South Africa	523	767	345	71	0.66	0.09
South Korea	569	684	398	62	0.70	0.09
Taiwan	388	829	388	29	1.00	0.03
Thailand	388	856	388	100	1.00	0.12
Turkey	271	261	271	144	1.00	0.55
Ukraine	372	422	372	48	1.00	0.11
United States	5,821	7,046	4,848	628	0.83	0.09
Venezuela	205	242	205	58	1.00	0.24
25 emitters	31,984	46,107	28,811	8,564	0.90	0.19
Rest of world industrial	515	540	423	77	0.82	0.14
Rest of world developing	3,436	6,549	3,436	4,683	1.00	0.72
World	35,935	53,196	32,671	13,323	0.91	0.25
Industrial	14,457	15,785	11,932	1,752	0.83	0.11
Developing	21,478	37,410	20,739	11,571	0.97	0.31

Source: Tables 2.2, 2.5, and D.1.

Table 5.2   Business as usual (bau) baseline and Copenhagen Convergence (CopCon) abatement path: Annual rates of growth in carbon plus energy efficiency ($w + c$) (percent)

Country/group	bau 2010–20	bau 2020–50	CopCon 2010–20	CopCon 2020–50	Increase 2010–20	Increase 2020–50
Argentina	3.06	2.08	3.06	6.06	0.00	3.98
Australia	2.61	2.37	5.65	9.47	3.04	7.11
Brazil	1.58	1.32	4.32	3.50	2.74	2.19
Canada	1.54	1.48	4.12	9.00	2.58	7.51
China	4.09	2.27	4.09	9.38	0.00	7.12
Egypt	2.63	1.44	2.63	2.70	0.00	1.27
European Union	1.78	1.67	3.69	7.13	1.92	5.47
India	3.42	2.67	3.42	3.73	0.00	1.05
Indonesia	2.18	1.15	5.19	2.98	3.01	1.84
Iran	1.57	0.98	1.57	7.90	0.00	6.93
Japan	0.62	0.69	4.25	6.26	3.63	5.57
Kazakhstan	3.33	2.44	3.48	10.48	0.15	8.04
Malaysia	2.84	1.78	2.84	9.29	0.00	7.51
Mexico	1.57	1.83	5.14	4.86	3.57	3.03
Pakistan	2.63	1.64	2.63	2.06	0.00	0.42
Russia	2.89	2.21	3.61	10.26	0.72	8.05
Saudi Arabia	1.97	1.67	1.97	9.87	0.00	8.20
South Africa	0.72	0.07	4.87	6.64	4.16	6.57
South Korea	3.44	1.78	7.01	8.59	3.57	6.81
Taiwan	1.33	0.26	1.33	11.46	0.00	11.20
Thailand	1.70	0.64	1.70	7.80	0.00	7.16
Turkey	2.83	2.55	2.83	4.53	0.00	1.98
Ukraine	2.35	1.69	2.35	8.93	0.00	7.24
United States	2.43	1.90	4.26	9.35	1.83	7.45
Venezuela	3.52	2.47	3.52	7.26	0.00	4.79
25 emitters	2.25	1.76	3.30	5.45	1.04	3.69
Rest of world industrial	2.05	1.74	4.02	7.59	1.97	5.86
Rest of world developing	2.06	1.88	2.06	3.33	–0.00	1.44
World	2.32	1.95	3.27	6.25	0.95	4.30
Industrial	1.96	1.72	3.88	8.41	1.92	6.69
Developing	2.78	2.12	3.13	5.92	0.35	3.79

Source: Tables 2.3, 2.4, D.1, and author's calculations.

The estimates of table 5.2 indicate that especially in the period 2020–2050, combined energy plus carbon efficiency growth would need to reach about 6 percentage points per year on average, or about three times as high as the 2 percent per year in the baseline. It seems likely that the great bulk of this acceleration would need to come from a massive shift away from fossil fuels as the source of energy. Relying primarily on increased energy efficiency would seem difficult, especially after exhaustion of an initial tranche of "free" energy savings. In comparison with baseline annual growth rates of about zero for energy output per unit of carbon (c, tables 2.3 and 2.4 in chapter 2), by implication this source of carbon saving would need to surge to perhaps 3 or even 4 percent per year. These estimates serve as a reminder that the challenge of global warming abatement is crucially one of identifying noncarbon sources of energy through major technological advances.

Abatement Costs under the Copenhagen Convergence Scenario

The Nordhaus RICE model, EMF-based, and McKinsey/Ackerman et al. cost curves discussed earlier can be used to translate the emissions cutbacks in table 5.3 into corresponding abatement costs. Table 5.3 first reports the central input into the cost calculations, the proportionate cut from the bau baseline for the country, and year in question in the CopCon abatement scenario.

Globally, emissions would decline from the bau baseline by a modest 9 percent in 2020 but then to more aggressive proportions of 35 percent in 2030, 57 percent in 2040, and 75 percent by 2050. By mid-century, industrial-country emissions would be 89 percent below the bau baseline. Somewhat more surprisingly, the cut would also be deep for developing countries, at 69 percent. The tendency to gauge cutbacks against 1990 base levels (as in the prominent UNDP targets) can leave the misleading impression that cutbacks for developing countries would be on the order of 20 percent, but instead their rapid economic and (for some) population growth mean that by 2050 their bau baselines would be so far above their 1990 starting points that the cutbacks would need to be deep. Indeed, with (weighted-) average cutbacks of 69 percent, their reductions from baseline would be approximately three-fourths as large as those of the industrial countries. These patterns suggest that by 2050, abatement costs in developing countries might be expected to be on the order of about one-half those of industrial countries, as a percent of GDP, other things being equal and applying the near-cubic cost function of the RICE model.[1]

Table 5.4 reports the corresponding abatement cost estimates by major country based on the RICE model cost parameters (table 4.1 in chapter 4). These costs are relatively modest. Globally they reach only about one-quarter percent of GDP by 2030, two-thirds of 1 percent by 2040, and 1.15 percent

---

1. That is, $(0.69/0.89)^{2.8} = 0.49$.

Table 5.3   Percent reduction in emissions from business as usual (bau) baseline, Copenhagen Convergence scenario

Country/group	2020	2030	2040	2050
Argentina	0	24	47	70
Australia	26	48	69	91
Brazil	24	39	51	61
Canada	23	47	70	92
China	0	39	68	88
Egypt	0	10	21	32
European Union	17	41	63	84
India	0	10	19	27
Indonesia	26	38	49	57
Iran	0	35	64	87
Japan	30	50	69	87
Kazakhstan	1	34	64	91
Malaysia	0	38	67	89
Mexico	30	46	60	72
Pakistan	0	3	7	12
Russia	7	40	68	92
Saudi Arabia	0	32	63	91
South Africa	34	57	76	91
South Korea	30	54	74	91
Taiwan	0	49	79	97
Thailand	0	42	70	88
Turkey	0	13	28	45
Ukraine	0	36	65	89
United States	17	40	65	91
Venezuela	0	24	49	76
25 emitters	10	38	62	81
Rest of world industrial	18	40	62	86
Rest of world developing	0	11	20	29
World	9	35	57	75
Industrial	17	42	65	89
Developing	3	31	53	69

Source: Calculated from tables 2.2, 2.5, and D.1.

Table 5.4   Abatement costs for the Copenhagen Convergence policy path: RICE model basis

Country/group	Percent of GDP				Amount (billions of 2005 ppp dollars)			
	2020	2030	2040	2050	2020	2030	2040	2050
Argentina	0.00	0.06	0.33	0.84	0.0	0.6	4.4	14.7
Australia	0.11	0.48	1.13	2.05	1.2	6.8	21.4	50.8
Brazil	0.07	0.22	0.41	0.57	2.0	9.3	23.5	45.2
Canada	0.08	0.46	1.16	2.09	1.2	9.1	28.2	61.6
China	0.00	0.36	1.29	2.13	0.0	94.8	518.1	1282.9
Egypt	0.00	0.01	0.03	0.09	0.0	0.0	0.3	1.1
European Union	0.03	0.23	0.66	1.26	4.2	45.8	155.4	349.6
India	0.00	0.01	0.04	0.09	0.0	0.8	6.0	19.6
Indonesia	0.16	0.39	0.62	0.81	2.4	8.5	20.0	37.4
Iran	0.00	0.23	1.04	2.14	0.0	2.9	16.6	42.1
Japan	0.17	0.55	1.12	1.82	7.6	25.3	51.4	82.0
Kazakhstan	0.00	0.18	0.85	1.84	0.0	0.7	4.0	11.2
Malaysia	0.00	0.37	1.52	2.83	0.0	3.7	23.3	65.8
Mexico	0.13	0.37	0.65	0.92	3.0	11.9	29.4	56.6
Pakistan	0.00	0.00	0.00	0.01	0.0	0.0	0.0	0.3
Russia	0.00	0.27	1.00	1.98	0.1	11.4	54.0	135.1
Saudi Arabia	0.00	0.19	1.01	2.42	0.0	2.6	19.4	64.0
South Africa	0.20	0.69	1.21	1.63	1.2	4.7	9.5	14.7

(continued on next page)

Table 5.4 Abatement costs for the Copenhagen Convergence policy path: RICE model basis *(continued)*

Country/group	Percent of GDP				Amount (billions of 2005 ppp dollars)			
	2020	2030	2040	2050	2020	2030	2040	2050
South Korea	0.16	0.70	1.39	2.03	3.2	17.9	45.2	81.0
Taiwan	0.00	0.75	2.37	3.50	0.0	10.1	42.2	79.6
Thailand	0.00	0.51	1.73	2.73	0.0	5.5	26.2	56.2
Turkey	0.00	0.01	0.07	0.22	0.0	0.1	1.4	5.7
Ukraine	0.00	0.22	0.90	1.70	0.0	1.2	6.3	14.6
United States	0.02	0.23	0.73	1.57	4.2	52.8	214.7	588.1
Venezuela	0.00	0.06	0.38	1.09	0.0	0.4	3.4	13.2
25 emitters	0.04	0.28	0.84	1.51	30.2	326.9	1,324.2	3,173.1
Rest of world industrial	0.04	0.29	0.85	1.73	0.8	7.7	26.9	64.5
Rest of world developing	0.00	0.01	0.04	0.09	0.0	2.8	19.7	63.3
World	0.03	0.22	0.66	1.15	31.0	337.4	1,370.9	3,300.9
Industrial	0.04	0.28	0.78	1.55	19.2	158.8	551.9	1,331.8
Developing	0.02	0.19	0.59	0.98	11.8	178.6	818.9	1,969.1

ppp = purchasing power parity

Source: Author's calculations based on tables 4.1 and 5.3.

by 2050. In view of the steep cutbacks from baseline by 2050, on the order of 90 percent even for many emerging-market economies, the limited abatement cost derives importantly from the reduction over time in the cost parameter as a consequence of improving technological alternatives.

As indicated in the table, as of 2020 abatement costs are extremely low at 0.04 percent of GDP for industrial countries and 0.02 percent for developing countries (although concentrated in a few of them). The low costs reflect the low initial costs for proportionately smaller cutbacks in the nearly cubic cost curve. Abatement costs for developing countries amount to only about $12 billion annually by 2020. By 2030, when all countries including developing countries are on a path of emissions reduction, the global cost rises to about $180 billion annually for developing countries, or about 0.2 percent of their combined GDP. China alone accounts for $95 billion, placing the estimate for all other developing countries at about $84 billion.

The estimates for developing-country abatement costs are modestly smaller if market exchange rates rather than purchasing power parity rates are used. A popular general form for converting between the two finds that the natural logarithm of the ratio of ppp value to market exchange rate value equals a constant plus a coefficient times the natural logarithm of ppp per capita income (see, e.g., Subramanian 2010). The World Bank (2010a, 379) reports that in 2008, for low-income countries ppp income per capita stood at $1,407 and market exchange rate income per capita at $524. The corresponding estimates for high-income countries were $39,345 and $37,141. A summary conversion function can be based on these two "observations."[2] Setting the ratio of market rate to ppp rate income at a maximum of unity, and applying the conversion, total abatement cost in 2030 remains unchanged for industrial countries but declines from $178.6 billion to $141.3 billion for developing countries. About three-fifths of the total reduction for developing countries is accounted for by China (with market rate costs of $72 billion versus ppp costs of $95 billion). For purposes of evaluating international financing needs, then, the difference between market and ppp exchange rate valuation by 2030 is not major, especially if China is unlikely to need financing.

As shown in table 5.5, application of the EMF 22–based cost estimates of appendix G and table 4.2 leads to considerably higher abatement costs, especially for developing countries. Thus, by 2030 global abatement costs are 1.33 percent of GDP ($2 trillion) instead of 0.22 percent ($337 billion; RICE basis, table 5.4). By 2050, global costs reach 2.92 percent of GDP, versus 1.15 percent. As exemplified in figure 4.1 in chapter 4, the divergence is greater for the developing countries, with 2050 abatement costs at 3.18 percent of GDP instead of 0.98 percent.[3]

---

2. Solving for two parameters with two observations, the result is that $\ln(\text{ppp}/r) = 3.0118 - 0.279 \ln y^*$, where ppp/r is the ratio of ppp income to market rate income and y^* is ppp income, dollars per capita.

3. It is also important to note that of the 10 models that ran stabilization scenarios in EMF 22,

Table 5.5 Abatement costs for the Copenhagen Convergence policy path: EMF 22 synthesis model basis

Country/region	Percent of GDP				Amount (billions of 2005 ppp dollars)			
	2020	2030	2040	2050	2020	2030	2040	2050
Argentina	0.00	1.21	2.70	3.68	0.0	12.4	36.2	63.8
Australia	0.44	1.06	1.64	1.81	4.6	14.9	30.9	44.8
Brazil	1.14	2.36	2.94	3.72	32.9	97.7	170.5	295.5
Canada	0.36	1.04	1.66	1.83	5.7	20.4	40.3	53.9
China	0.00	2.42	5.39	6.35	0.0	638.1	2,166.7	3,819.5
Egypt	0.00	0.37	0.64	0.91	0.0	2.9	6.6	11.7
European Union	0.27	0.80	1.24	1.89	45.0	159.8	295.3	523.3
India	0.00	0.25	0.63	1.05	0.0	25.2	95.3	234.6
Indonesia	1.38	2.39	2.88	2.61	20.3	52.6	92.8	119.8
Iran	0.00	2.08	4.61	5.49	0.0	26.4	73.6	108.3
Japan	0.55	1.14	1.62	1.67	25.0	52.3	74.4	75.4
Kazakhstan	0.02	2.02	4.65	5.91	0.1	7.3	22.0	36.0
Malaysia	0.00	2.34	5.07	5.72	0.0	23.1	77.6	132.8
Mexico	1.69	3.11	4.16	3.87	37.9	100.1	187.8	239.1
Pakistan	0.00	0.05	0.09	0.16	0.0	0.6	1.6	4.4
Russia	0.17	2.44	4.31	6.48	5.7	103.3	231.9	441.2
Saudi Arabia	0.00	1.89	4.52	5.94	0.0	25.6	86.6	157.3
South Africa	2.01	4.19	6.29	5.87	12.0	28.7	49.2	52.6

South Korea	1.69	3.90	6.07	5.88	32.8	99.8	197.5	234.7
Taiwan	0.00	3.33	6.70	6.53	0.0	44.9	119.3	148.7
Thailand	0.00	2.73	5.49	5.59	0.0	29.9	83.3	115.1
Turkey	0.00	0.16	0.37	0.57	0.0	2.6	8.0	15.2
Ukraine	0.00	0.71	1.49	1.73	0.0	4.0	10.4	14.8
United States	0.29	1.18	1.40	2.07	51.6	268.0	410.3	774.3
Venezuela	0.00	1.23	2.95	4.31	0.0	8.3	27.0	52.2
25 emitters	0.32	1.59	2.93	3.69	273.5	1,849.2	4,595.1	7,769.3
Rest of world industrial	0.25	0.81	1.38	1.64	5.4	21.5	44.1	61.2
Rest of world developing	0.00	0.41	0.62	0.76	0.0	128.6	300.2	555.9
World	0.26	1.33	2.37	2.92	278.9	1,999.3	4,939.4	8,386.3
Industrial	0.31	1.11	1.60	2.30	142.9	640.2	1,127.1	1,974.2
Developing	0.22	1.47	2.77	3.18	136.0	1,359.1	3,812.2	6,412.1

ppp = purchasing power parity

Source: Author's calculaltions based on tables 4.2 and 5.3.

As discussed in appendix G, however, the same EMF 22 model compilation included carbon price estimates with global trading, and these can be interpreted as a ceiling that would be placed on marginal costs of abatement. Ironically, the result would be that many developing countries would be purchasing emissions rights from industrial countries rather than the usually expected reverse pattern, because of the generally higher marginal abatement costs in developing regions in the EMF compilation (examined further later). Appendix G shows that if the median global carbon prices in the 450 ppm scenarios in EMF 22 are applied as ceilings to marginal abatement costs, the cost estimates fall substantially for developing countries. For China, for example, the cost of meeting the CopCon abatement target in 2050 falls from 6.35 percent of GDP to 4.11 percent. For all developing countries, the cost in 2050 falls from 3.18 percent of GDP to 2.02 percent (table 5.5 and table G.2 in appendix G). Globally, abatement costs in 2030 fall from 1.33 percent of GDP to 0.64 percent (and from $2 trillion to $966 billion).

At the other end of the cost spectrum, table 5.6 reports the corresponding CopCon abatement cost estimates for 2030 using the McKinsey/Ackerman et al. cost curves, which are available only for that date and are specified at market rather than ppp exchange rates.

The McKinsey-based abatement cost estimates for 2030 are only about one-third as high as those using the Nordhaus RICE model cost parameters, with the world total cost at $123 billion versus $337 billion, respectively. The share of developing countries in global abatement costs is moderately less in the McKinsey-based estimates (48.1 percent, table 5.6) than in those based on RICE model parameters (52.9 percent, table 5.4).[4] The estimate of $59 billion abatement cost for developing countries at market exchange rates of constant 2005 dollars in 2030 compares with a market rate estimate of $154 billion on the RICE parameter basis (just discussed). For China, the market rate comparison identifies abatement costs of $31 billion using the McKinsey cost functions versus $72 billion using the market rate conversion of the RICE parameter–based estimate.

The McKinsey-based estimates here are broadly consistent with estimates reported in McKinsey (2009, 8). The McKinsey authors call for a reduction in global emissions to 35 percent below the 1990 level by 2030, or by 70 percent below the bau baseline they project for 2030. With global CO_2 emissions at 21.9 $GtCO_2$ in 1990 (table 2.2), this target would place emissions at 14.2 $GtCO_2$ in

---

only 2 were able to achieve a ceiling of 450 ppm CO_2-e without temporary overshooting (Clarke et al. 2009, S68). As noted above, the CopCon scenario implies 437 ppm CO_2 and 476 ppm CO_2-e by 2050, somewhat less ambitious than the EMF 22 target. In addition, several of the models may have applied either higher baseline emissions or climate subroutines generating higher atmospheric retention, or assumed higher relative weights of non-CO_2 gases.

4. By 2030, developing countries also account for more than half of world GDP, and by a wider difference ($93 trillion at 2005 ppp dollars for developing countries, versus $58 trillion for industrial countries).

Table 5.6 Abatement costs in 2030 for the Copenhagen Convergence policy path: McKinsey/Ackerman et al. basis

Country/group	Percent of GDP	Amount (billions of 2005 dollars)
Argentina	0.02	0.2
Australia	0.26	3.6
Brazil	0.09	3.8
Canada	0.28	5.5
China	0.12	31.3
Egypt	0.00	0.0
European Union	0.12	24.9
India	0.00	0.3
Indonesia	0.08	1.7
Iran	0.13	1.7
Japan	0.17	7.6
Kazakhstan	0.08	0.3
Malaysia	0.10	0.9
Mexico	0.08	2.6
Pakistan	0.00	0.0
Russia	0.07	2.9
Saudi Arabia	0.08	1.1
South Africa	1.08	7.4
South Korea	0.09	2.4
Taiwan	0.21	2.9
Thailand	0.17	1.9
Turkey	0.01	0.1
Ukraine	0.09	0.5
United States	0.07	17.0
Venezuela	0.03	0.2
25 emitters	0.10	120.6
Rest of world industrial	0.09	2.4
Rest of world developing	0.00	0.0
World	0.08	123.0
Industrial	0.11	63.8
Developing	0.06	59.1

Source: Author's calculations based on tables 4.3 and 5.3.

2030, a reduction of 66 percent from the bau baseline estimated in the present study (41.4 GtCO$_2$; table 2.2). The McKinsey authors indicate a global abatement cost of €200 billion to €350 billion annually by 2030 (euros of 2005). The CopCon abatement path considered here would place global emissions at 26.8 GtCO$_2$ in 2030 (table D.1 in appendix D), a cutback of 35 percent from baseline. With the depth of cut from baseline nearly twice as great in the McKinsey *Pathways* study as in the main scenario considered here, it is to be expected that the global abatement costs projected for 2030 would be on the order of twice as large (or more) as those calculated here despite the use of the same underlying abatement cost functions.

To recapitulate, the three sets of estimates show a wide range of abatement costs for the CopCon scenario. For 2030, global abatement costs range from only $123 billion (0.08 percent of world product) using the McKinsey-based parameters and $337 billion (0.22 percent) for the RICE model parameters to a much higher $2.0 trillion (1.33 percent) using the EMF-based parameters (but with a more moderate $966 billion, or 0.64 percent of world product, using the EMF parameters with the global carbon price applied as a ceiling on marginal cost).

Other Model–Based Estimates

It is useful to consider other model estimates of abatement costs generally and two recent estimates specifically for the Copenhagen Accord outcome.

At the general level, the IPCC (2007b) has summarized cost estimates of numerous climate-economic models for alternative target ranges for stabilizing CO$_2$-e. It places the 10th percentile to 90th percentile global cost estimates for 540 ppm CO$_2$-e at 0 to 2 percent of world product in 2030 and 0 to 3 percent in 2050 (p. 204). For category III stabilization (535 to 590 ppm CO$_2$-e), it places the median model estimate at cost of 0.6 percent of world product in 2030 and 1.3 percent in 2050. For more ambitious category I (445 to 490 ppm CO$_2$-e) and category II (490 to 535 ppm CO$_2$-e) stabilization, the IPCC (2007b) reports that the model estimates are below 3 percent of world product in 2030 and below 5.5 percent in 2050, but it also notes that the models achieving this degree of abatement tend to use the lower baselines among the array of bau projections (pp. 205–06). For the specific model estimates for which it gives detail, five models show an average cost of 0.66 percent of world product in 2030 for a 490 ppm stabilization path; for 2050, eight models (including three with relatively higher emissions baselines) show 490 to 535 ppm stabilization cost at an average of 2.3 percent of world product (ranging from 0.1 to 5 percent; IPCC 2007b, p. 205, figure 3.25).

The 2030 estimate in table 5.4 for the CopCon policy is global abatement cost of 0.22 percent of world product. Nordhaus (2010a) reports that his model uses "a cost function for CO$_2$ emissions that is drawn from more detailed models at the national and regional levels from the IPCC Fourth Assessment Report [IPCC 2007b] and the Energy Modeling Forum 22 report

[Clarke et al. 2009]" and hence is designed to be representative of the main climate-energy models.

For the United States, the Congressional Budget Office (CBO 2009) reports a range of cost estimates for the cuts subsequently offered by the United States in the Copenhagen Accord: 17 percent below 2005 levels by 2020 and 83 percent below 2005 levels by 2050. The CBO's preferred abatement cost range is from 0.25 to 0.75 percent of GDP in 2020 and from 1.0 to 3.5 percent by 2050 (p. 11). In comparison, the RICE model parameters used here calculate costs of 0.02 percent of GDP in 2020 and 1.57 percent in 2050 (table 5.4). The model's cost equations thus are lower than the CBO's preferred range for the initial phase but well within it by 2050, likely reflecting the sharply nonlinear form of the RICE cost function.[5]

For the Copenhagen Accord, new estimates by Nordhaus (2010a, 11725, figure 4) are broadly consistent with the estimates of the present study. This need not be the case, because although Nordhaus uses the same cost functions, his baseline emissions are not necessarily the same as the projections based on the Energy Information Administration and their extensions here. Nordhaus estimates abatement costs for the United States at about 0.05 percent of GDP in 2025 and 0.9 percent in 2055. The corresponding estimates for the European Union are about 0.09 and 0.7 percent. In comparison, the comparable with-trade estimates in the present study (RICE model basis) are 0.01 percent of GDP in 2020 and 1.54 percent in 2050 for the United States, and respectively 0.02 and 1.20 percent for the European Union.[6] So the cost estimates here are modestly higher by 2050 than those in Nordhaus (2010a) for these two cases.[7]

Far more pessimistic abatement cost estimates for the Copenhagen Accord are calculated by McKibben, Morris, and Wilcoxen (2010), using their G-Cubed general equilibrium model. They estimate that by 2020 the Copenhagen Accord abatement pledges would impose costs amounting to 2.7 percent of GDP for the United States, 4.9 percent of GDP for Western Europe, 3.7 percent for China, and 3.2 percent for the world as a whole (p. 28). These costs are about an order of magnitude higher than even the highest 2020 costs estimated here (EMF basis, table 5.5). A small part of the divergence stems from their substan-

---

5. Note, however, that the same report indicated that the "range from other studies" was from –0.15 percent of GDP (i.e., savings) to 2.0 percent in 2020 and from 0.8 to 4.6 percent in 2050 (CBO 2009, 11).

6. Table 5.4 costs minus the savings from trade in table 6.2.

7. Comparison of the estimates here with those in Nordhaus (2010a) are less meaningful for his other regions, because other countries typically did not specify goals by 2050. Nordhaus postulates high-income countries make cuts similar to the US proposals "with developing countries following in the next 2 to 5 decades" (p. 11723), but does not cite specific paths. By 2055 his abatement costs stand at 0.9 percent for China and Latin America and 0.95 percent for India. In contrast, the 2050 cost estimates here are significantly higher for China, somewhat lower for Latin America, and much lower for India (tables 5.4 and 6.2). The difference for India likely reflects the adoption here of convergence to equal per capita emissions, combined with India's low starting point for per capita emissions.

tially higher emissions baseline, which reaches 49 GtCO$_2$ globally in 2020 (p. 38) instead of 35.9 GtCO$_2$ in the present study (table 2.2). Correspondingly, there are considerably deeper cuts to reach the 2020 targets: 33 percent below baseline for the United States instead of 17 percent, and 36 percent instead of 17 percent for the European Union. The authors have a cut from baseline of 22 percent for China by 2020, in sharp contrast to the interpretation in this study that there is no cut from baseline.

A more important source of the high cost estimates, however, comes from a much higher cost for any given percent cutback from baseline. Thus, instead of 2.7 percent of GDP, the 2020 cost of a 33 percent cut from bau for the United States would be only 0.16 percent of GDP using the RICE model cost function (table 4.1) and 0.86 percent using the EMF-based function (table 4.2). If the RICE cost parameters are applied to each country and the McKibben-Morris-Wilcoxen abatement cuts are evaluated, the result is a global abatement cost at 0.10 percent of world product, instead of 3.2 percent. Perhaps in part because of its unusual features mixing macroeconomic equations (such as money demand functions) with sectoral energy coefficients, the model does not seem to be representative of the mainstream models in the principal surveys (IPCC 2007b, Clarke et al. 2009, CBO 2009).

Alternative Abatement Paths

Three alternatives to the central CopCon abatement path warrant consideration. Each represents a different mixture of equity objectives and practicality. Appendix D reports the emissions paths for each of the 25 major economies under each of the alternative emissions abatement paths considered.

UNDP (2007)

The United Nations Development Program (UNDP 2007, 48) has called for an aggressive abatement program designed to give a 50 percent chance of holding global warming at no more than 2°C above preindustrial levels. For this purpose, by 2050 global emissions would be cut to one-half of their 1990 levels. This cut would be accomplished by reductions of at least 80 percent from the 1990 levels by industrial countries and 20 percent from 1990 levels by developing countries. As an interim target, industrial countries would cut emissions by at least 30 percent from 1990 levels by 2020. Emissions of developing countries would continue to rise until 2020, but would then begin their descent to 20 percent below 1990 levels by 2050.

The UNDP path is consistent with targets announced by the main industrial countries in the Copenhagen Accord for 2050. However, the path is more aggressive than pledged for 2020 by the United States in particular, reflecting the fact that US emissions by 2007 had risen about 19 percent above the 1990 level, whereas for the European Union emissions were about 4 percent below

1990 levels (in part because of cutbacks in formerly Eastern European economies that had joined the European Union).

In the implementation of the stylized UNDP proposal here, there is an
important exception to the 20 percent cut from 1990 levels for developing
countries: the case of rest of world "other" developing countries not included
in the 25 large economies directly examined. Many poor countries in Africa
and South Asia are in this residual category, and they account for a large
aggregate population: 1.7 billion in 2007 and 3.3 billion in 2050 (table A.1).
Per capita emissions for this group were only 1.1 $GtCO_2$ in 2007. Their aggregate emissions in 1990 were 2.0 $GtCO_2$. A 20 percent reduction from this level
combined with the rise in the group's population would cut per capita emissions to only 0.49 tCO_2 by 2050, only about one-third the global average in the
main CopCon scenario. To preserve the spirit of the UNDP proposal without
forcing this extreme result, it is simply assumed that per capita emissions of
this group remain unchanged at 1.1 tCO_2 by 2050, still considerably below the
global average but by a more plausible margin.

Chakravarty et al. (2009)

A second alternative scenario, proposed by Chakravarty et al. (2009), is
premised on the argument that emissions reductions should be based on
reducing high emissions by individuals, not countries. The proposal essentially recognizes that there is an international middle class that includes a relatively large group of households in such countries as China, India, and Brazil,
and that such households should participate in global emissions reductions
despite the modest levels of countrywide per capita incomes in their countries.
The authors use income distribution data for individual countries to identify a
global distribution of CO_2 emissions by individuals. They can then identify the
ceiling on emissions per individual, wherever located, consistent with future
global emissions targets. As an example, they note that if global emissions were
limited to 13 $GtCO_2$ annually for 2030, caps limiting emissions would affect
1.13 billion high-emitting individuals, roughly equally distributed among four
groups: the United States, the OECD countries other than the United States,
China, and non-OECD countries other than China (p. 1). Appendix D provides
further detail on implementation of the Chakravarty et al. policy path.

Frankel (2008)

A third alternative abatement proposal has been developed by Frankel (2008).
His policy path is based on a combination of politics, economics, and ethics.
He seeks to observe three main principles. First, developing countries are not
asked to bear any cost in the early years. Second, thereafter they are not asked to
make any sacrifice "different in kind" from those made by any country that has
begun abatement earlier, "with allowance for differences in incomes." Third, no

country is asked to accept an ex ante target that costs it more than 1 percent of the present value of future GDP, or more than 5 percent of GDP in any single period. To implement this scheme he identifies a Progressive Reductions Factor, a Latecomer Catch-Up Factor, and a Gradual Equalization Factor. After experimenting with alternative parameters for each of these factors, he identifies a path that limits atmospheric concentration to 500 ppm by 2100. Appendix D provides additional detail on implementation of the Frankel emissions paths.

Figure 5.2 shows the alternative policy paths for carbon dioxide emissions by developed and developing countries from 2010 through 2050. For the developed countries the alternatives are relatively similar, although the early cutbacks are considerably less severe in the central CopCon path and the Chakravarty et al. and Frankel paths than in the UNDP path. The divergences are greater for the developing countries. The Frankel path allows continued absolute increases through 2050. The Chakravarty et al. path, available only through 2030, similarly allows absolute increases. In contrast, the CopCon and UNDP paths call for substantial reductions for developing countries after 2020, with deeper cuts for these countries in the UNDP path than in the CopCon scenario.

Table 5.7 provides country detail to contrast the 2050 targets under the central CopCon scenario and the UNDP scenario. Whereas the UNDP approach provides uniformity in one dimension—an equal percent cut from the 1990 level for industrial countries and another, much lower equal percent cut for all developing countries—the CopCon scenario gives uniformity in a more basic dimension, per capita emissions levels by the target date of 2050 (1.43 tCO_2 per person, whether in an industrial or developing country). The result is a relatively wide dispersion of results in the dimension not chosen in the scenario in question. In the CopCon scenario, the percent change from 1990 ranges from about a 90 percent reduction for the main industrial countries (as well as Russia and Ukraine) to a 477 percent *increase* in the case of Pakistan, as well as sizable increases for India, Indonesia, and the "rest of world developing" group. The comparison between India and China is particularly important. With convergence to an equal per capita level of emissions by 2050, the consequence is to reduce total absolute emissions by 16 percent from the 1990 level for China but increase it by 243 percent for India.

In contrast, in the UNDP scenario, it is the target 2050 per capita emissions levels that, as the dimension not chosen for harmonization, winds up being extremely diverse. The US level is about 20 percent higher than the EU level. India winds up with a target of only 0.33 tCO_2 per capita, whereas China is allowed about four times as much per capita. Kazakhstan and Ukraine are allowed about 14 tCO_2 per capita because of their extremely high starting points and their treatment as developing countries reducing emissions only 20 percent from the 1990 base.

For the world as a whole, the CopCon scenario is somewhat less ambitious than the UNDP scenario, with a cut of 39 percent from 1990 levels rather than 47 percent. Industrial countries as a group cut emissions 87 percent from the

Figure 5.2   Alternative policy paths for CO_2 emissions, 2010–50

a. Developed countries

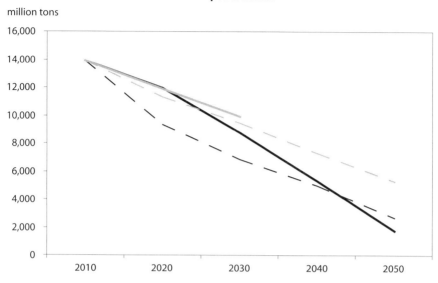

b. Developing countries

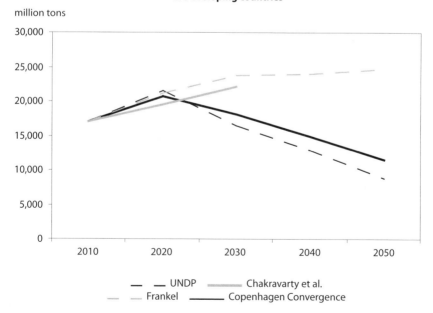

Source: Appendix D.

Table 5.7 2050 emissions under Copenhagen Convergence (CopCon) and UNDP scenarios

Country/group	Percent change from 1990 levels by 2050		Emissions per capita (tCO$_2$)		
				2050	
	CopCon	UNDP	2007	CopCon	UNDP
Argentina	−32	−20	4.3	1.43	1.68
Australia	−86	−80	18.1	1.43	2.02
Brazil	78	−20	1.8	1.43	0.64
Canada	−87	−80	16.1	1.43	2.19
China	−16	−20	5.0	1.43	1.36
Egypt	160	−20	2.5	1.43	0.44
European Union	−84	−80	8.3	1.43	1.83
India	243	−20	1.4	1.43	0.33
Indonesia	197	−20	1.8	1.43	0.38
Iran	−49	−20	7.3	1.43	2.23
Japan	−89	−80	9.7	1.43	2.50
Kazakhstan	−92	−20	12.8	1.43	13.85
Malaysia	9	−20	10.0	1.43	1.05
Mexico	−45	−20	4.1	1.43	2.08
Pakistan	477	−20	0.9	1.43	0.20
Russia	−92	−80	11.2	1.43	3.80
Saudi Arabia	−67	−20	15.3	1.43	3.45
South Africa	−79	−20	9.0	1.43	5.40
South Korea	−74	−20	9.9	1.43	4.46
Taiwan	−77	−20	11.5	1.43	5.00
Thailand	4	−20	4.7	1.43	1.10
Turkey	−2	−20	3.9	1.43	1.16
Ukraine	−92	−20	6.9	1.43	14.57
United States	−87	−80	19.3	1.43	2.22
Venezuela	−53	−20	5.9	1.43	2.43
25 emitters	−56	−60	5.6	1.43	1.31
Rest of world industrial	−75	−80	12.5	1.43	1.12
Rest of world developing	134	80	1.1	1.43	1.10
World	−39	−47	4.5	1.43	1.24
Industrial	−87	−80	12.2	1.43	2.18
Developing	35	3	2.8	1.43	1.09

UNDP = United Nations Development Program

Source: UNDP (2007); author's calculations.

Table 5.8 Cumulative CO$_2$ emissions after 2010 and atmospheric concentrations

Scenario	2020	2030	2040	2050
Cumulative emissions (billion tons)				
Business as usual baseline	334	721	1,164	1,665
Copenhagen Convergence	318	616	851	1,019
UNDP (2007)	309	579	786	933
Chakravarty et al. (2009)	312	629		
Frankel (2008)	317	646	968	1,275
Atmospheric concentration (parts per million CO$_2$)				
Business as usual baseline	407	431	460	494
Copenhagen Convergence	405	421	432	437
UNDP (2007)	404	418	426	429
Chakravarty et al. (2009)	405	423		
Frankel (2008)	405	424	443	460

Source: Author's calculations.

1990 level (rather than 80 percent), whereas developing countries in the aggregate are allowed an increase of 35 percent rather than a decrease of 3 percent (the latter reflecting a 20 percent decrease from 1990 for all developing countries except the large "rest of world developing" bloc—which turns out to be allowed an 80 percent *increase* to accommodate its large increase in population).

Table 5.8 shows the corresponding cumulative emissions and atmospheric concentrations for each of the four alternative paths, along with those for the bau baseline for comparison. The atmospheric concentrations are calculated using the method presented in appendix B.

The abatement costs of the alternative policy paths, as a percent of GDP, are reported in appendix E, using the Nordhaus RICE cost functions. For industrial countries, in the UNDP scenario abatement costs are somewhat higher in the first three decades but somewhat lower by 2050 than in the central CopCon scenario. These costs for 2020, 2030, 2040, and 2050 are 0.26 percent of GDP, 0.61 percent, 0.89 percent, and 1.3 percent (table E.1 in appendix E), rather than 0.04 percent, 0.28 percent, 0.78 percent, and 1.55 percent (table 5.4), respectively. For developing countries the abatement costs are higher in the UNDP scenario already by 2030 (0.30 percent of GDP versus 0.19 percent, reaching 1.33 percent of GDP by 2050 instead of 0.98 percent). Abatement costs are lower in the Chakravarty et al. and Frankel paths than in either the CopCon or UNDP paths, reflecting the less ambitious cuts (see figure 5.2). Thus, by 2050 global abatement costs are only 0.45 percent of world GDP (table E.3), versus 1.15 percent in the CopCon scenario (table 5.4) and 1.32 percent in the UNDP scenario (table E.1).

6

Trade and Timing

Globally efficient emissions reductions would differ from the country-specific time paths of emissions reductions in the Copenhagen Convergence (CopCon) scenario. Countries with lower marginal abatement costs would cut by more, and others by less, with trading of emissions rights accounting for the differences. Reallocation of emissions cuts over time, toward more aggressive cuts by 2020 and more moderate cuts than otherwise required by 2040, would also reduce global abatement costs. The country- and region-specific cost functions can be used to identify the differences in marginal abatement costs, and optimization can be used to find the best combination of trading across countries and reallocation of cuts across time.

Trading turns out to reduce global abatement costs, but by less than might seem intuitive. For industrial countries, by 2030 emissions trade cuts abatement cost by 0.02 percent of GDP, less than one-tenth of the abatement cost of 0.28 percent of GDP without trading. Using the intermediate RICE model cost functions, for all countries, the present value of cost for abatement that meets the CopCon total emissions over the next 40 years amounts to 0.45 percent of the present value of world product for this period (discounting at a low 1.5 percent and less when discounting at higher rates). The cost can be cut to 0.40 percent of world product by allowing trading across countries and cut further to 0.33 percent of world product by reallocating cuts over time. Instead of reducing global emissions from baseline by only 9 percent in 2020, they would be cut by 26 to 32 percent (depending on the discount rate), permitting a less severe cut from baseline in 2040 (by 39 to 45 percent instead of 57 percent).

By 2030, international carbon trade amounts to about 0.75 billion tons of carbon dioxide ($GtCO_2$) per year, or about 3 percent of global emissions along the CopCon abatement path. The carbon price by then is $54 per ton of carbon dioxide (RICE model basis, in 2005 dollars), similar to the $40 estimated by the Congressional Budget Office for the Waxman-Markey bill of 2009 (CBO 2009). In general, industrial countries would purchase emissions rights from developing countries, with key exceptions. Relatively ambitious targets for Brazil, Mexico, and South Korea would make them purchasers rather than sellers, and by 2030 China would shift from being a large seller to a large purchaser.

Overall the findings indicate that even without trade and earlier cutbacks, abatement costs should be of a manageable order of magnitude (0.39 percent of present value of world product from 2010 to 2050, discounting at 3 percent and using the RICE model; 1.4 percent using the EMF 22–based cost functions). Cost can be cut by about one-tenth through trading and by about one-fourth if in addition the cuts from baseline are smoothed toward earlier cuts.

Shadow Price of Carbon Dioxide

The central CopCon scenario for carbon dioxide abatement is essentially premised on a combination of political feasibility on the one hand and equity on the other, with a greater emphasis on feasibility in the first decade in view of the actual pledges in the Copenhagen Accord and on equity in the subsequent three decades as emissions per capita converge to a uniform global level. It is unlikely that this set of country emissions paths will be the most efficient from the standpoint of a global planner seeking to minimize abatement cost subject to the constraint of meeting the same declining path of aggregate world emissions. In some countries the marginal cost of abatement will be higher than in others, and global costs will be reduced if trading of emissions rights enables the first group to accomplish some of their target reductions in emissions by purchasing additional abatement in the second group. In the terminology of cost-benefit analysis, each country's marginal cost of abatement can be seen as the "shadow price" of carbon dioxide applicable to the economy in question.[1] In principle, policy decisions, such as what pattern of trading in emissions rights to pursue, would be evaluated on the basis of these shadow prices.

To consider this issue, it is necessary to examine the marginal cost of abatement by country along the target abatement paths. This marginal cost can be calculated from the Nordhaus-RICE abatement cost function of equation 4.1 as follows. With k as the ratio of total carbon abatement cost to GDP, or $k = C/Y$ where C is total carbon abatement cost for the year in question and Y is GDP, and ignoring the year subscript, total abatement cost will then be:

$$C = kY = Y\alpha\mu^\beta \qquad (6.1)$$

---

1. This study does not attempt to estimate the marginal social benefit of abatement, for example, using the discounted future flow of damages avoided. Estimating such damages and, especially, incorporating possible catastrophic damages is a difficult task that will not be revisited in the present study (see Cline 1992, 2010a). Instead, for the purposes here the CopCon international abatement target path is taken as given and the shadow price becomes the marginal abatement cost needed to achieve it.

Considering the definition of μ as the proportionate cutback in emissions from baseline, defining ΔE as the absolute reduction and E as the baseline level of emissions, this can be rewritten as:

$$C = Y\alpha \left(\frac{\Delta E}{E}\right)^{\beta} = \frac{Y\alpha}{E^{\beta}} (\Delta E)^{\beta} \tag{6.2}$$

Marginal cost of abatement will then be:

$$\frac{dC}{d(\Delta E)} = \frac{\beta Y\alpha}{E^{\beta}} (\Delta E)^{\beta - 1} \tag{6.3}$$

For example, for the United States in 2020, absolute reduction in emissions from baseline amounts to ΔE = 973 million tCO_2, baseline emissions are E = 5,821 million tCO_2, and GDP at 2005 purchasing power parity (ppp) dollars is $17.5 trillion. With α = 0.036 for 2020 (RICE model basis, table 4.1 in chapter 4) and β =2.8, equation 6.3 works out to $12 per ton of CO_2. This shadow price is in the same broad range as the $22 per ton identified by the Congressional Budget Office (CBO 2009, 11) as the price for emissions allowances by 2020 in a rising path consistent with meeting the abatement goals in the Waxman-Markey bill passed by the US House of Representatives (but not the Senate), which had the same targets as in the US Copenhagen Accord submission.

Table 6.1 reports the shadow prices of carbon dioxide, or marginal costs of abatement, by country and year in the CopCon policy scenario and without trading of emissions rights. These estimates apply equation 6.3. The first set of estimates uses the RICE model cost parameters of table 4.1; the second applies the EMF-based parameters of table 4.2. The marginal cost estimates assume that each country achieves its target cutbacks solely from reductions in its own emissions, rather than partly through purchasing "carbon offsets" involving extra emissions reductions by countries from whom the offsets are purchased.

As would be expected, the absence of abatement targets by 2020 for many developing countries, including China and India, means that in that year their marginal cost of abatement is zero. However, the major emerging-market economies that have undertaken Copenhagen Accord cutbacks from baseline (Brazil, Indonesia, Mexico, South Africa, and South Korea) do have significant marginal costs, typically in the range of $50 per ton of carbon dioxide in the RICE function and far higher ($250 to $400) in the EMF-based functions. Somewhat surprisingly, these marginal costs are higher than those in the main industrial countries, even in the RICE functions. Considering that the RICE cost parameter is typically about the same for the two sets of countries (for example, in 2020 α = 0.038 for Brazil and Mexico [Latin America] and 0.036 for the United States, table 4.1), the explanation is paradoxically that the cutbacks from baseline are more ambitious in these major emerging-market economies than in the industrial countries. Thus, Mexico's cutback from baseline is 30 percent whereas the cutbacks for the European Union and the United States are 17 percent (table 5.3 in chapter 5).

Table 6.1   Shadow price of CO_2 under Copenhagen Convergence abatement in the absence of international offsets trading (2005 ppp dollars/metric ton of CO_2)

Country/group	RICE cost basis				EMF 22 synthesis basis			
	2020	2030	2040	2050	2020	2030	2040	2050
Argentina	0	31	109	233	0	327	566	640
Australia	31	92	189	329	64	106	158	167
Brazil	47	105	165	221	410	603	570	690
Canada	24	83	163	259	60	97	135	130
China	0	57	148	237	0	188	351	399
Egypt	0	5	17	34	0	170	209	226
European Union	17	76	167	284	81	121	163	219
India	0	9	31	62	0	159	248	376
Indonesia	54	98	139	174	232	306	407	351
Iran	0	32	88	145	0	147	245	234
Japan	55	118	188	258	95	127	156	137
Kazakhstan	0	23	73	141	27	128	250	285
Malaysia	0	76	210	350	0	242	440	445
Mexico	59	128	208	295	378	543	840	785
Pakistan	0	1	5	14	0	129	120	148
Russia	2	44	121	220	70	221	248	343
Saudi Arabia	0	38	121	235	0	187	341	364
South Africa	19	39	52	59	96	119	170	133

South Korea	52	147	255	365	272	414	703	665
Taiwan	0	113	226	278	0	252	402	327
Thailand	0	71	155	208	0	194	311	268
Turkey	0	12	52	137	0	109	171	209
Ukraine	0	24	66	109	0	42	63	64
United States	12	58	139	257	83	166	110	140
Venezuela	0	21	83	199	0	221	411	498
Rest of world industrial	25	100	221	390	85	146	208	213
Rest of world developing	0	16	50	95	0	376	478	525

ppp = purchasing power parity

Source: Author's calculations; see text.

To examine how much global abatement costs can be reduced by allowing trading in emissions rights, it is possible to conduct a cost minimization calculation that allows each country either to buy or to sell tons of carbon dioxide subject to the constraint that for each year in question there is no change from the CopCon global emissions target.[2] Table 6.2 reports the results of this exercise when applying the RICE cost function.[3]

Using the RICE cost parameters, the pattern of trading is broadly as expected. The United States, European Union, and Japan are large purchasers of emissions rights; developing countries are generally sellers, with especially large sales by India. China is a key exception. Although its lack of pledged cutbacks from the bau baseline in 2020 means that it is a large seller of emissions in that year, by 2030 and after its CopCon abatement targets are so stringent against a rapidly rising bau baseline that it becomes the largest purchaser of emissions rights. In addition, Brazil, Mexico, and South Korea are important purchasers as a consequence of their ambitious CopCon scenarios.

Total trade in emissions amounts to about 1 billion tons per year in the first three decades and 1.4 billion by 2050. The global shadow price of carbon dioxide, and hence the market-clearing price, is only $4.8 per ton in 2020, but it rises rapidly to about $54 by 2030, $128 by 2040, and $218 by 2050.[4] The estimate for 2030 is relatively close to the allowance price of $40 estimated for that year by the Congressional Budget Office (CBO 2009) for the United States under the Waxman-Markey bill of 2009. The annual value of emissions trading would be only about $6 billion in 2020 but $39 billion by 2030, $110 billion by 2040, and $306 billion by 2050.

The reductions in abatement costs accomplished through emissions trading are moderate and decline over time in proportionate terms. For the world as a whole, abatement costs are reduced from $30 billion in 2020, $337 billion in 2030, $1.37 trillion in 2040, and $3.3 trillion in 2050 to, respectively, $6 bil-

---

2. This minimization is carried out using the Solver routine in Microsoft Excel.

3. The trading results obtained applying the EMF-based cost functions are not reported because of their relatively implausible and unstable patterns, reflecting much higher marginal abatement costs for developing countries as well as shifts in cost function exponents from one period to the next. For example, in 2030 the European Union not only meets its own abatement target of a 41 percent cut from baseline—a cut of 1.69 $GtCO_2$—but also cuts an additional 2.2 $GtCO_2$ to sell to the international emissions trading market. The United States makes small purchases in 2030 but by 2040 the drop in its cost function exponent shifts it to a large seller of emissions rights (2.0 $GtCO_2$).

4. The cost minimization calculation constrains emissions cutbacks to no more than 95 percent of bau baseline levels to avoid the outcome of negative net emissions available for national use (emissions rights sales in excess of total baseline emissions). This constraint becomes binding for South Africa by 2040 and additionally for Iran, Kazakhstan, and Ukraine by 2050, so marginal cost in these countries and periods is somewhat lower than the market-clearing international shadow price. Note that in the trade experiment using the EMF-based cost functions (not reported), the global marginal cost path is higher, especially initially, at $72/tCO_2$ in 2020, $161 in 2030, $280 in 2040, and $400 in 2050.

lion, $278 billion, $1.22 trillion, and $3.02 trillion. Emissions trading thus cuts global costs by 80 percent from a low base in 2020, 18 percent in 2030, 11 percent in 2040, and 8 percent in 2050. The larger scope for cost reductions in 2020 reflects the absence of target cuts for China, India, and most other developing countries, such that these countries have a cushion of low-cost abatement opportunities available for sales to industrial countries. The subsequent decline in emissions trading gains reflects the tightening CopCon abatement trajectory for most developing countries over time.

For the industrial countries the CopCon scenario without trading incurs abatement costs averaging only 0.04 percent of GDP in 2020 (RICE cost basis), but rising to 0.28 percent in 2030, 0.78 percent in 2040, and 1.55 percent in 2050 (table 5.4). The savings from trade amount to about 0.02 to 0.03 percent of their GDP in the first three periods and 0.05 percent by 2050. By 2050, then, emissions trading reduces abatement costs for industrial countries by only about 3 percent. Consider the case of the United States in 2050. Its cutback from baseline by 91.1 percent would cost 1.57 percent of GDP (table 5.4). Its purchases of 562 million tCO_2 would enable the cutback to be moderated to 83 percent from baseline, curbing the abatement cost to 1.21 percent of GDP. However, its cost of emissions rights purchases at $218 per ton would amount to $122 billion per year or 0.33 percent of GDP (about $37 trillion by then). The net savings would amount to: 1.57 – 1.21 – 0.33 = 0.03 percent of GDP. Trading would thus reduce abatement costs by only about 2 percent.

These calculations suggest that the widespread perception of large abatement cost reductions for industrial countries through emissions trading with developing countries may have been overstated.[5] The trading gains are proportionately large only in 2020 when the industrial-country abatement costs are low. In that year costs for industrial countries can approximately be cut in half by emissions trading. By 2040, in contrast, abatement costs are considerably higher, but with the high shadow price of carbon dioxide the trading price is also higher and purchases are expensive, providing little net gain (0.78 percent of GDP domestic abatement costs for industrial countries without trading, table 5.4; savings of only 0.03 percent of GDP from trading, table 6.2). Another indication of the limited gains from trading by 2030–50 is the relative similarity of abatement costs without trading as a percent of GDP for industrial versus developing countries (table 5.4). The closer these two cost fractions are, the less scope there will be for reducing abatement costs in high-cost industrial countries through the purchase of emissions rights that have less scarcity value in lower-cost developing countries.

---

5. In the Waxman-Markey legislation passed by the US House of Representatives in 2009, up to 2 billion tCO_2 in reductions of annual emissions levels were allowed to come from offsets, of which up to three-fourths could be international. In contrast, in the results for 2030–40 in table 6.2, annual US purchases of international assets are an average of only about 150 million tCO_2, and by 2050, only about 560 million tCO_2. The implication is that the relative cheapness of offsets purchased from abroad assumed in framing the legislation was considerably greater than estimated here.

Table 6.2 Purchases (+) or sales (−) of CO_2 emissions rights, global shadow price, and savings from emissions trading: RICE cost function basis

Country/group	Trade (million tons of CO_2 per year)				Savings (percent of GDP)			
	2020	2030	2040	2050	2020	2030	2040	2050
Argentina	−18	−20	−11	7	0.01	0.02	0.01	0.00
Australia	68	54	62	89	0.07	0.07	0.10	0.19
Brazil	88	77	52	6	0.05	0.05	0.02	0.00
Canada	81	66	61	61	0.04	0.05	0.04	0.04
China	−936	139	747	691	0.02	0.00	0.02	0.01
Egypt	−20	−66	−116	−167	0.01	0.23	0.72	1.35
European Union	354	299	354	476	0.01	0.02	0.03	0.06
India	−146	−407	−655	−881	0.01	0.10	0.23	0.33
Indonesia	91	70	18	−79	0.13	0.07	0.00	0.04
Iran	−70	−82	−123	−70	0.02	0.07	0.16	0.04
Japan	286	213	146	80	0.13	0.14	0.09	0.04
Kazakhstan	−28	−48	−58	−9	0.03	0.21	0.36	0.01
Malaysia	−21	24	74	122	0.01	0.03	0.19	0.34
Mexico	106	100	93	84	0.11	0.11	0.08	0.05
Pakistan	−12	−58	−116	−188	0.00	0.15	0.46	0.81
Russia	−82	−78	−40	11	0.00	0.01	0.00	0.00
Saudi Arabia	−52	−42	−15	32	0.02	0.03	0.00	0.01
South Africa	96	−67	−129	−32	0.10	0.07	0.22	0.01

South Korea	125	146	157	155	0.13	0.25	0.29	0.28
Taiwan	-29	85	141	103	0.01	0.18	0.37	0.13
Thailand	-34	32	48	-19	0.01	0.02	0.04	0.00
Turkey	-22	-46	-49	-34	0.01	0.06	0.09	0.05
Ukraine	-52	-77	-117	-27	0.03	0.21	0.55	0.02
United States	389	120	183	562	0.01	0.00	0.00	0.03
Venezuela	-22	-37	-32	-9	0.01	0.09	0.08	0.01
Rest of world industrial	55	63	89	128	0.02	0.05	0.12	0.28
Rest of world developing	-195	-461	-764	-1,091	0.00	0.03	0.07	0.10
World	-0	0	0	0	0.02	0.04	0.07	0.10
Industrial	1,150	736	854	1,407	0.02	0.02	0.03	0.05
Developing	-1,150	-736	-854	-1,407	0.02	0.05	0.10	0.12
Shadow price (2005 ppp dollars per ton)	4.8	53.6	128.3	217.6				

Source: Author's calculations; see text.

Finally, it should be noted that a few developing countries do wind up with relatively large trading gains by 2050. Emissions rights sales generate net savings of 1.35 percent of GDP for Egypt, about 0.8 percent for Pakistan, and about 0.3 percent for India.

A striking feature of the estimates is that the international shadow price is low in 2020 but rises exceptionally rapidly thereafter. The rise from $4.8 per ton in 2020 to $53.6 in 2030 is at an astonishing annual rate of 24 percent. The shadow price rises at an annual rate of 9 percent from 2030 to 2040 and at 5.4 percent from 2040 to 2050.[6] The strong implication is that international abatement could be made considerably more efficient through the redistribution of cutbacks toward the earlier part of the period. In principle the shadow price of carbon should rise at the so-called social rate of time preference, the rate at which future consumption should be discounted in project analysis. For very long term problems such as global warming over two centuries or more, in Cline (1992) I have argued that this rate should be on the order of 1.5 percent per year; Nordhaus (2008) places the rate at about 5 percent over the next 50 years.[7] So a more efficient abatement strategy would generate a path of shadow prices for carbon dioxide rising at 5 percent annually or less, instead of far higher.

Appendix F reports the results of analyzing the cost-efficient profile of carbon abatement over time by applying alternative discount rates, allowing each year's reductions from the bau baseline to vary from the CopCon scenario but constraining the cumulative sum of emissions reductions for 2010–50 to the same total as in the CopCon policy path. In addition, the cost minimizations impose the constraint that global emissions in 2050 must equal those in the CopCon scenario; otherwise the reallocation of abatement toward lower-cost 2020 could leave unsustainably high emissions in 2050.[8] As shown in the appendix, when reallocation is allowed across periods, the time path of the global shadow price of carbon is much smoother than in the base case of CopCon abatement. On the basis of the estimates in appendix F, table 6.3 summarizes the alternative profiles of emissions over time under five variants of the CopCon policy scenario, with aggregates at the level of industrial and developing countries as well as detail for the United States and China. The five variants are: the version with no trade; the version with trade across countries but fixed world targets for each year in question; and three cost-minimizing

---

6. The corresponding path of the shadow price using the EMF cost functions has annual increases of 8.0 percent in 2020–30, 5.5 percent in 2030–40, and 3.6 percent in 2040–50.

7. The social rate of time preference equals the rate of pure time preference (for impatience), plus the so-called elasticity of marginal utility multiplied by the growth rate of per capita consumption. Cline (1992) and Stern (2007) place pure time preference at zero; Nordhaus (2008), at 1.5 percent. Cline and Stern place the elasticity of marginal utility at 1.5 and 1.0, respectively; Nordhaus, at 2.

8. Implicitly the target of uniform global per capita emissions at 1.4 $GtCO_2$ in the CopCon scenario is meant to yield a path consistent with observing the 450 ppm ceiling without requiring a sharp, discontinuous further drop in emissions after 2050.

Table 6.3 Global CO$_2$ emissions under alternative variants of the Copenhagen Convergence (CopCon) policy scenario (GtCO$_2$)

Country/group	Business as usual	CopCon	With trade	With period reallocation at[a] 1.5 percent	With period reallocation at[a] 3 percent	With period reallocation at[a] 5 percent
			2020			
World	35.9	32.7	32.7	24.3	25.4	26.7
Industrial	14.5	11.9	13.1	9.6	10.0	10.6
United States	5.8	4.8	5.2	3.7	3.9	4.2
Developing	21.5	20.7	19.6	14.7	15.4	16.1
China	9.5	9.5	8.6	6.2	6.5	6.9
			2030			
World	41.4	26.8	26.8	26.7	26.9	27.2
Industrial	15.0	8.8	9.5	9.4	9.5	9.6
United States	6.2	3.7	3.8	3.8	3.8	3.9
Developing	26.4	18.1	17.3	17.2	17.4	17.6
China	11.9	7.2	7.3	7.3	7.4	7.5
			2040			
World	47.1	20.3	20.3	28.8	27.5	25.9
Industrial	15.4	5.3	6.2	9.2	8.8	8.2
United States	6.6	2.3	2.5	3.8	3.6	3.4
Developing	31.7	14.9	14.1	19.6	18.8	17.7
China	14.4	4.6	5.4	8.3	7.9	7.3
			2050			
World	53.2	13.3	13.3	13.3	13.3	13.3
Industrial	15.8	1.8	3.2	3.2	3.2	3.2
United States	7.0	0.6	1.2	1.2	1.2	1.2
Developing	37.4	11.6	10.2	10.2	10.2	10.2
China	17.2	2.0	2.7	2.7	2.7	2.7

a. Discount rate.

Source: Table 6.2; appendix F; author's calculations.

versions that additionally allow reallocation of abatement over time, corresponding to three discount rates. All five variants constrain 2050 emissions to the same global total as in the initial CopCon scenario.

When reallocation over time is permitted, the effect is to reduce emissions in 2020 so that they can be used later. In practice, the result is that the cost minimization outcome leaves emissions practically unchanged in the intermediate year of 2030 (and also by construction in the end-period year of 2050) but takes away emissions from 2020 and transfers them to 2040. Comparison of the reallocation-scenario shadow price paths (appendix F) against that without reallocation shown in table 6.2 confirms that the broad effect of flexibility in timing is to transfer some of the emissions otherwise permitted in 2020 to the year 2040, as the shadow price jumps sharply for 2020 (from $4.8 per ton to $47 per ton) and declines significantly in 2040 (from $128 to $64).[9]

As expected from the steep path of the carbon dioxide shadow prices in table 6.1 (RICE basis), allowing redistribution of abatement over time results in more aggressive cutbacks in 2020 than under the Copenhagen Accord. Even discounting at the high rate of 5 percent, global emissions in 2020 would be constrained to 26.7 $GtCO_2$ instead of the 32.7 $GtCO_2$ level of the Copenhagen Accord, widening the cut from the bau baseline from 9 to 25.6 percent. With the discount rate at 1.5 percent per year, the cost-efficient 2020 target would be even more ambitious, with emissions at 24.3 $GtCO_2$, a cut of 32.3 percent from the bau baseline. Globally efficient abatement would similarly call for more aggressive cutbacks from baseline by the United States (36.2 percent reduction discounting at 1.5 percent, versus 17 percent) and China (34.7 percent versus zero).

Two considerations could moderate the implication that more front-end-loading would be required for efficient global abatement. The first would be that the cost parameters used for the calculation might be overly optimistic toward the early end of the horizon (or unduly pessimistic for the later periods). In particular, the ratio of marginal cost in 2020 to that in 2030 is much lower in the RICE functions than in the EMF-based functions (table 6.1). The second would be simpler: The body politic is simply not prepared to move as aggressively and as soon as called for by least-cost abatement, so the excess cost of a slower start should be seen as the price of not being able for political reasons to act in the most efficient manner. This interpretation would be a case of the classic problem of the best becoming the enemy of the good, in the sense that insistence on the earlier and more cost-effective abatement might jeopardize political acceptance of any action at all.

Table 6.4 reports the discounted present value of abatement costs for the alternative variants of the CopCon policy scenario. Because these are totals over 40 years, they are large in absolute terms. Thus, discounting at 1.5 percent per year, the present value of abatement costs globally amounts to about $21 trillion (2005 ppp dollars) without trading, $18 trillion with trading, and $15 trillion if reallocation across periods is allowed to smooth out marginal costs over time. With the highest discount rate considered, 5 percent, the corresponding estimates are $7 trillion, $6 trillion, and about $5 trillion, respectively. The corresponding present value figures for global product are far larger, however, ranging from $4,540 trillion discounting at 1.5 percent to $2,285 trillion at 5 percent. The resulting present values of abatement costs turn out to be quite modest as fractions of the present value of GDP. Thus, for the world as a whole,

---

9. Discounting at 1.5 percent per year. However, the shadow price still jumps to $218 in 2050 when the stringent end-period per capita emissions target must be met.

Table 6.4   Present value of abatement costs under alternative Copenhagen Convergence (CopCon) scenarios: RICE cost basis

	Country/ group	CopCon	With trade	With reallocation at[a] 1.5 percent	With reallocation at[a] 3 percent	With reallocation at[a] 5 percent
			Trillions of dollars			
1.5 percent	World	20.6	18.2	14.8		
	Industrial	8.5	6.2	5.1		
	United States	3.4	2.8	2.3		
	Developing	12.1	12.0	9.7		
	China	7.6	6.4	5.1		
3 percent	World	12.8	11.2		9.3	
	Industrial	5.3	3.9		3.3	
	United States	2.1	1.7		1.5	
	Developing	7.5	7.4		6.1	
	China	4.6	3.9		3.2	
5 percent	World	7.0	6.0			5.2
	Industrial	2.9	2.1			1.8
	United States	1.1	0.9			0.8
	Developing	4.0	4.0			3.4
	China	2.5	2.1			1.8
			Percent of GDP			
1.5 percent	World	0.45	0.40	0.33		
	Industrial	0.50	0.37	0.30		
	United States	0.51	0.42	0.34		
	Developing	0.43	0.42	0.34		
	China	0.94	0.79	0.64		
3 percent	World	0.39	0.34		0.28	
	Industrial	0.42	0.30		0.26	
	United States	0.42	0.35		0.29	
	Developing	0.37	0.36		0.30	
	China	0.81	0.69		0.56	
5 percent	World	0.31	0.26			0.23
	Industrial	0.32	0.23			0.20
	United States	0.32	0.27			0.23
	Developing	0.29	0.29			0.25
	China	0.65	0.55			0.46

a. Discount rate.

Source: Author's calculations; see text.

with discounting at 1.5 percent per year, abatement costs range from 0.45 to 0.33 percent of the present value of world product. At the high discount rate, the range is even lower, at 0.23 to 0.31 percent. (Note that in the variants allowing reallocation of the global target across years, only the solution that applies the discount rate in question is relevant.)

The present value cost estimates are broadly similar for industrial and developing economies. The cost estimates confirm that China in particular can benefit from greater front-end-loading of abatement, as its 40-year present value of abatement costs falls from 0.94 percent of GDP under CopCon without trading or reallocation to 0.64 percent with trading and reallocation, discounting at 1.5 percent. The gains from earlier action hold up even with the high discount rate, falling from 0.65 to 0.46 percent of GDP discounting at 5 percent.

Although the experiments of abatement reallocation over time and resulting present values are not calculated for the EMF-based cost functions—for the same reasons noted above for not applying these functions in the trading experiment—those cost functions would yield considerably higher estimates for the present value of abatement costs. Thus, for the simple CopCon policy without trading or reallocation over time, corresponding to the first column in table 6.4, the present value of abatement costs using the EMF functions and a 3 percent discount rate amounts to $46.3 trillion instead of $12.8 trillion, or 1.4 percent of the present value of world product for 2010–50 instead of 0.39 percent. The comparison would be somewhat higher than this ratio of 3.6:1 for the other experiments (i.e., the remaining columns in the table), because of lesser scope for gains from reallocation over time with a relatively higher marginal cost early in the horizon. Even so, it is useful to note that even without trading or reallocation toward earlier action, the high end of the abatement cost range of the three broad sets of models considered in this study places the present value of aggressive abatement at less than 1½ percent of world GDP for 2010–50.

Overall, the estimates in table 6.4 strongly suggest that more ambitious abatement targets by 2020 could substantially reduce total eventual abatement costs. Reallocation of some of the cutbacks from the 2040s to the 2020s would reduce total costs by about one-fifth (for example, from about 0.40 percent of the present value of world product to 0.33 percent, discounting at 1.5 percent). Trading is also important to minimizing abatement costs, as it permits a reduction of about 10 percent in the total (from 0.45 to 0.40 percent of the present value of world product, discounting at 1.5 percent).

7

Estimating Investment Requirements and Adaptation Costs

International official estimates of investment needed to curb global warming tend to be high. The International Energy Agency has estimated that to adhere to a limit of 450 parts per million (ppm) for carbon dioxide–equivalent atmospheric concentration, additional energy-related investment over 2010–30 would need to reach about $10.5 trillion, or about 0.5 percent of world product in the two decades. However, saving from reduced annual fuel requirements would offset about four-fifths of the total. Similarly, the World Bank (2010a) cites McKinsey estimates to conclude that upfront investment costs are about three times as high as economic costs of abatement.

In contrast, a simple model developed in this chapter suggests that the annual investment cost associated with prospective economic costs of abatement should be only about 40 percent as large as the abatement costs. The intuition is that abatement cost is an annual flow whereas the capital needed is a stock. Application of reasonable capital-output ratios to arrive at an increase of capital necessary to compensate the estimated abatement cost and provide for subsequent depreciation yields this lower relationship of annual investment cost to annual economic abatement cost. The investment cost model is then applied to the set of alternative abatement cost estimates under the Copenhagen Convergence (CopCon) scenario to arrive at corresponding annual investment costs over 2020–30 and 2030–40. For the two preferred abatement cost models, RICE and EMF 22 "constrained," global investment costs would amount to about 0.15 percent of world product in the first decade and 0.3 percent in the second. For developing countries, the annual investment for abatement amounts to about $90 billion in 2020 and $300 billion in 2030. Excluding China, the 2020 total stands at about $40 billion.

For adaptation requirements (for example, in agriculture, infrastructure, coastal defense, and health), consideration of the two principal official studies suggests that costs in developing countries could be on the order of $50 billion annually in 2020, or about $33 billion excluding China, Korea, Malaysia, and Taiwan for purposes of assessing plausible financing needs.

International Energy Agency

The International Energy Agency (IEA 2009b) prepared analysis prior to the United Nations Framework Convention on Climate Change (UNFCCC) negotiations at Copenhagen in December 2009, setting forth a scenario for international actions through 2030 that would place the world on a path to limit atmospheric concentration of greenhouse gases to 450 ppm of CO_2-equivalent. The analysis identifies sectors, technologies, and regions in which the emissions cutbacks could occur and develops corresponding estimates of investment costs. In this scenario, energy-related CO_2 emissions peak in about 2020 at 30.9 billion tons (Gt) and fall to 26.4 Gt by 2030 versus 40 Gt in the IEA's 2030 "reference" business as usual (bau) path. This path is similar to the CopCon scenario (without reallocation over time) examined here, which places these emissions at 32.6 Gt in 2020 and 26.8 Gt in 2030.[1]

The IEA envisions introduction of a carbon price by 2013 in the "OECD+" countries (including non-OECD EU countries) in power and industry and industrial-sector agreements in non-OECD countries. The power sector would account for 70 percent of emissions reductions (IEA 2009b, 221). Energy-efficiency measures and higher electricity prices would reduce demand. By 2030 renewables would account for 37 percent of global electricity production, nuclear 18 percent, and coal with carbon capture and sequestration (CCS) 5 percent. Coal-based power would fall by 50 percent from the reference path. The transport sector would account for one-eighth of global CO_2 emissions cutbacks and three-fourths of the reductions in oil, on the basis of a decline in conventional internal combustion engines to 40 percent instead of 90 percent in the reference scenario and a sharp increase in hybrids and electric vehicles. In industry, emissions would be about one-fourth lower than in the baseline, with the cutbacks concentrated in iron, steel, and cement. In this scenario, perhaps politically the most challenging component would be the sharp reduction in coal, reflecting the relatively minor prospect envisioned for CCS by 2030.

The IEA estimates additional energy-sector investment of $10.5 trillion globally over 2010–30 in order to achieve the 450 ppm CO_2-equivalent scenario's emissions path, back-end-loaded with three-fourths of the increment occurring in the 2020s (p. 257). Of the total, $5 trillion would be in OECD countries, $3.1 trillion in major emerging-market economies, and $1.9 trillion in other

---

1. The bau baseline here, 41 $GtCO_2$ by 2030 (table 2.2), is also similar to the IEA reference path estimate of 40 $GtCO_2$.

developing countries. Annual additional investment needs would amount to $430 billion or 0.5 percent of GDP in 2020 and $1.15 trillion or 1.1 percent of GDP in 2030. The sectoral composition of incremental investment for 2010–30 is as follows: $4.8 trillion in transport (mainly for buying hybrid and electric cars), $2.6 trillion in buildings, $1.8 trillion in power plants, $1.1 trillion in industry, and $400 billion in biofuels. In power, the incremental investment amounts to 28 percent above baseline investment, bringing the 20-year total (including baseline) to $8 trillion. The estimates imply that reducing emissions is considerably cheaper in power than in transport. Transportation and biofuels would account for 50 percent of the incremental investment but provide only 30 percent of emissions reductions. The other 50 percent of incremental invest-ment in power (the power sector directly plus buildings plus industry) would provide 70 percent of the emissions reductions.

The IEA also estimates that there would be $8.6 trillion in savings on energy bills in transport, buildings, and industry over 2010–30 and $17 trillion in investment-lifetime savings. Oil and gas import bills for the OECD coun-tries would be much lower than in the reference case and about 30 percent lower in China and India. The IEA estimates thus imply that for 2010–30 as a whole, the net costs of abatement would be $1.9 trillion (i.e., $10.5 trillion minus $8.6 trillion). This amount would correspond to only about one-tenth of 1 percent of world product over the period (approximately $2,000 trillion based on tables A.1 and A.2 in appendix A). This is in the same order of magni-tude as estimated here using the RICE cost functions and lower than the esti-mate based on the EMF cost function. Thus, for the CopCon scenario even without trading, global abatement cost (RICE basis) rises from zero in 2010 to 0.03 percent of world product by 2020 and 0.22 percent by 2030 (table 5.4 in chapter 5). By implication the average net abatement cost for 2010–30 would amount to 0.07 percent of world product, close to the 0.1 percent in the IEA analysis.[2] In contrast, the EMF-based cost would average 0.46 percent of GDP, about four times the IEA net cost estimate.[3]

The IEA estimates highlight the large gap between investment cost and economic cost. For 2010–30 as a whole, the incremental investment of $10.5 trillion (about 0.5 percent of world product for the period) is five times as large as the net economic cost after energy savings. The relationship of invest-ment cost to economic cost is particularly important in considering financing requirements and is considered further later.

The IEA study also provides specific estimates for financing needs. In its 450 ppm CO_2-equivalent scenario, in 2020 the annual incremental investment requirements in non-OECD countries amount to $197 billion, of which Russia accounts for $8 billion and China $80 billion. Other major emerging-market economies account for $34 billion, and other developing countries $73 billion

---

2. Taking the average of 0.015 percent in 2010–20 and 0.125 percent in 2020–30; table 5.4.

3. That is, an average of 0.13 percent in 2010–20 and 0.80 percent in 2020–30; table 5.5.

(IEA 2009b, 295). CO_2 emissions trading could account for a sizable amount of financing, the study finds, with such trade between the OECD countries and other regions amounting to 0.5 $GtCO_2$ to 1.7 $GtCO_2$ annually by 2020. With a central estimate for the carbon dioxide price at about $30 per ton, annual trading could amount to about $40 billion (p. 293).

World Bank

For its part, the World Bank (2010a) devoted the late-2009 issue of its annual *World Development Report* (WDR) to climate change policy. The WDR estimated that annual costs to keep the world on a path to 450 ppm CO_2-equivalent would amount to 0.3 to 0.9 percent of world GDP by 2030 (p. 198). In comparison, the CopCon estimate is 0.22 percent of world product using the RICE model cost parameters (table 5.4), and only 0.08 percent using the McKinsey-based parameters (table 5.6), but 1.33 percent using the EMF-based cost functions (table 5.5). The WDR places the marginal cost at $35 to $100 per ton of CO_2 by 2030, broadly consistent with the $54 per ton global shadow price calculated here using the RICE function (table 6.2 in chapter 6). The corresponding global mitigation costs would be $425 billion to $1 trillion annually by 2030. The lower end of this range is broadly comparable to the $337 billion estimated here using the RICE cost parameters (table 5.4); the upper end is consistent with the "alternate" version of the EMF-based cost estimates ($966 billion; table G.2 in appendix G).

The World Bank study emphasizes that because of "high up-front capital costs followed later by savings in operating cost" (p. 259), financing requirements can be considerably higher than lifetime costs. It cites unpublished estimates of McKinsey & Company placing annual mitigation costs for developing countries at $175 billion and corresponding investment costs at $563 billion annually by 2030 (p. 260), for a relationship of 3 to 1 for investment relative to annual economic cost.[4] However, in the underlying McKinsey source, and in the variant treating the initial negative-cost opportunities at zero cost (the approach consistent with the form of equations 4.2 and 4.3 in chapter 4), the cost was higher and the investment/economic cost ratio stood at 1.8 in 2030 (McKinsey 2009, 39, 43).

The report cites annual mitigation investment costs for 2030 from four sources: IEA, McKinsey, MESSAGE model, and REMIND model.[5] The respective estimates at the global level are $846 billion, $1.01 trillion, $571 billion, and $424 billion. The corresponding respective estimates for developing

---

4. The relationship should depend on the profile of investment over time, however, and in general should fall over time unless there is a continuous acceleration of new investment. Otherwise the cumulative delayed savings would rise relative to the cost for each new cohort of investment.

5. The latter two models are, respectively, those of the International Institute for Applied Systems Analysis and Potsdam Institute for Climate Impact Research.

countries are $565 billion, $563 billion, $264 billion, and $384 billion.[6] Of the developing-country totals, detail from the McKinsey estimates attributes 47 percent to China and 13 percent to India; the MESSAGE model, 19 percent for China and 16 percent for India (p. 199).

Investment Levels Implied by Abatement Cost Estimates

The estimates of abatement costs as a percent of GDP by benchmark future years can be translated into corresponding estimates of investment needed over time. Suppose that at year $t+10$, a decade from the year in question, abatement cost is projected at k_{t+10}, as a percent of GDP. Suppose in the base year t abatement cost is k_t. The investment program seeks to maintain the capital built up previously to compensate for abatement costs by year t, plus additional investment to address the increase in abatement costs expected by the end of the decade. In most developing countries, the capital-output ratio is on the order of 2 or 3 to 1. Let the capital-output ratio be Γ. Then in order to offset the loss of output amounting to k_{t+10}, the amount of capital needed 10 years from now would be Γk_{t+10}, expressed as a percent of GDP 10 years from now. An investment program during the coming decade that will accomplish this buildup in capital can be calculated as:

$$I_t = \frac{1}{10}(k_{t+10} - k_t)\Gamma(1 + g + n)^5 \left(\frac{1}{1-\frac{1}{L}}\right) + \frac{\Gamma}{L}k_t \tag{7.1}$$

Here, I_t is extra investment needed in year t as a percent of GDP, g and n are growth rates of per capita GDP and population as before, and L is average capital life in years. The initial term, one-tenth, reflects the fact that there is a time horizon of 10 years to accumulate the extra capital needed by year $t+10$. The term Γ is required to go from product flows (abatement cost or output loss) to capital stock. The next to last term in parentheses is a scale factor that takes account of the fact that average economic scale in the decade will be higher than in the initial year (with GDP growth to the fifth year taken into account). The next term is essentially a decay factor that amounts to setting aside funds for capital depreciation. If average capital stock life is 15 years, the investment flows need to be expanded by the factor $1/[1-1/15] = 1.071$. The final, separate additive term is the amount of investment needed to take care of annual depreciation of the capital stock already built up to offset abatement costs by the beginning of the period.

Consider the case of China in 2030. Using the RICE cost function, by 2040 abatement cost under the CopCon scenario will amount to 1.29 percent of GDP. In 2030 the cost is already 0.36 percent of GDP, and capital will have been built up to offset this cost. But the increase of 1.29 - 0.36 = 0.93 percent of GDP will have to be dealt with. The investment program beginning in 2030 to

---

6. McKinsey (2009, 40, 43) instead reports annual investment in 2030 at $811 billion globally and $463 billion for developing countries. The reason for the higher World Bank figures is unclear.

offset extra capital costs by 2040 will then be: $I = 1/10 \times 0.93\% \times 3 \times (1+.0425 - .0005)^5 \times (1.071) = 0.367\%$, using a capital-output ratio of Γ=3. In addition, the annual depreciation on the capital stock built up already by 2030 will be $(3/15) \times 0.36\% = 0.072\%$. The total annual investment needed to offset the increment in abatement costs expected by 2040, in 2030 and every year during the decade, will thus be 0.439 percent of GDP.

A key finding in this formulation of the problem is that unless the initial abatement costs are extremely low relative to the cost that will be reached a decade or so in the future, annual investment needs are likely to be smaller, rather than larger, than the annual abatement costs. This conclusion is somewhat counterintuitive, particularly because of the general concept of "upfront" investment costs versus long streams of subsequent payoffs. But it follows simply from the fact that the capital required is a stock whereas the abatement cost is a flow (perhaps most easily thought of as forgone production or income annually). There are 10 years of annual increments of capital stock to prepare for the abatement cost flow at the end of the decade. If capital is infinitely lived, and there is no further increase in abatement costs as a percent of GDP, then no further investment will be needed (except to keep pace with GDP scale). By implication, the ratio of 2 or 3 for annual investment costs to economic abatement costs identified by McKinsey for 2030 may be overstated.

Table 7.1 applies equation 7.1 to the four cost estimates from the present study to obtain estimates of investment requirements for abatement during the decades 2020–30 and 2030–40. The McKinsey-based function of table 5.6 is available only for the first decade.[7] (The estimates use Γ=3.)

As shown in the table, there is a wide range of estimates for investment needed for abatement, ranging from 0.03 to 0.46 percent of world product in 2020–30. Even the high end (EMF basis) is lower than the average of 0.5 percent of world GDP in 2020 and 1.1 percent in 2030 estimated by the IEA as discussed above. For the decade 2030–40 the investment requirement stands higher in each of the variants but is still less than two-thirds of 1 percent of GDP even in the highest estimate.

Table G.3 in appendix G reports the corresponding estimates in terms of absolute dollar values (in constant 2005 dollars at purchasing power parity). For 2020 global investment requirements range from \$32 billion to \$495 billion, with the corresponding range for developing countries being from \$15 billion to \$333 billion. The two preferred models of this study are the RICE-cost basis and the EMF-alternate basis. Averaging the two, the preferred estimate of global investment needs stands at \$164 billion in 2020 and \$464 billion in 2030. The corresponding amounts for developing countries are \$94 billion in 2020 and \$294 billion in 2030. The latter estimate is close to the low end of the range of four models cited by the World Bank as noted above (\$264 billion, MESSAGE

---

7. Note moreover that because there is no McKinsey-based estimate for abatement cost in 2020, the calculation here assumes that the average ratio of the cost (as a percent of GDP) in 2020 to that in 2030 as estimated by the RICE and EMF functions also applies to the McKinsey function.

Table 7.1 Annual investment required for Copenhagen Convergence abatement, 2020–40 (percent of GDP)

Country/group	McKinsey/ Ackerman et al.	2020–30 RICE	EMF	EMF- alternate	2030–40 RICE	EMF	EMF- alternate
Argentina	0.01	0.02	0.45	0.15	0.11	0.79	0.33
Australia	0.08	0.16	0.32	0.21	0.34	0.43	0.36
Brazil	0.03	0.07	0.70	0.14	0.11	0.69	0.25
Canada	0.09	0.15	0.31	0.21	0.34	0.43	0.48
China	0.05	0.14	0.97	0.49	0.44	1.66	0.89
Egypt	0.00	0.00	0.14	0.07	0.01	0.17	0.16
European Union	0.04	0.08	0.24	0.14	0.19	0.32	0.24
India	0.00	0.00	0.10	0.06	0.01	0.20	0.12
Indonesia	0.02	0.12	0.67	0.23	0.17	0.67	0.43
Iran	0.05	0.08	0.76	0.46	0.34	1.33	1.04
Japan	0.05	0.16	0.30	0.20	0.29	0.38	0.33
Kazakhstan	0.03	0.07	0.74	0.48	0.28	1.37	1.04
Malaysia	0.04	0.15	0.95	0.41	0.53	1.55	0.80
Mexico	0.02	0.12	0.88	0.18	0.18	1.02	0.33
Pakistan	0.00	0.00	0.02	0.01	0.00	0.02	0.03
Russia	0.02	0.10	0.85	0.41	0.32	1.17	0.68
Saudi Arabia	0.03	0.07	0.71	0.37	0.35	1.38	0.86

(continued on next page)

Table 7.1 Annual investment required for Copenhagen Convergence abatement, 2020–40 (percent of GDP) *(continued)*

Country/group	2020–30				2030–40		
	McKinsey/Ackerman et al.	RICE	EMF	EMF-alternate	RICE	EMF	EMF-alternate
South Africa	0.31	0.21	1.15	0.76	0.32	1.56	1.47
South Korea	0.03	0.23	1.15	0.30	0.39	1.57	0.56
Taiwan	0.08	0.28	1.25	0.52	0.75	1.91	1.08
Thailand	0.06	0.19	1.04	0.53	0.56	1.59	1.08
Turkey	0.00	0.00	0.06	0.04	0.02	0.11	0.09
Ukraine	0.03	0.08	0.25	0.25	0.29	0.42	0.42
United States	0.03	0.08	0.38	0.23	0.23	0.32	0.39
Venezuela	0.01	0.02	0.46	0.21	0.13	0.89	0.48
25 emitters	0.04	0.10	0.54	0.27	0.27	0.81	0.50
Rest of world industrial	0.03	0.10	0.25	0.15	0.25	0.36	0.28
Rest of world developing	0.00	0.00	0.17	0.05	0.01	0.17	0.09
World	0.03	0.08	0.46	0.22	0.21	0.62	0.38
Industrial	0.04	0.09	0.35	0.20	0.24	0.39	0.35
Developing	0.02	0.07	0.54	0.23	0.20	0.74	0.39

Sources: McKinsey-Ackerman: table 5.6; RICE: table 5.4; EMF: table 5.5; EMF-alternate (constrained EMF): table G.2.

model). Within the developing-country totals, the investment requirement for China alone amounts to $53 billion in 2020 and $176 billion in 2030 (preferred estimate averaging the RICE and EMF-alternate results). Investment occurs already in 2020 for China despite the absence of any cutback in emissions from baseline in 2020. This reflects the decadal investment program needed to be launched already by 2020 in order to build up capital to offset the abatement costs expected by 2030. If China is set aside as not needing outside financing because of its large external reserves, then the remaining investment requirements for emerging-market and developing countries amount to $41 billion in 2020 and $118 billion in 2030 (again using the average of the two preferred models).

Adaptation

Costs for adaptation to unavoidable global warming constitute a second area of prospective needs for international finance. The principal recent estimates of adaptation costs are from the secretariat of the UNFCCC (2007) and the World Bank's Economics of Adaptation to Climate Change (EACC) team (World Bank 2010b). The World Bank calculated annual costs for adaptation in developing regions for 2010 through 2050 (at constant 2005 dollars) at an annual average of $75 billion to $100 billion. Somewhat surprisingly, the "wet" climate model (NCAR) turned out to have higher adaptation costs than the "dry" one (CSIRO) because of higher infrastructure costs in East Asia and the Pacific under the wetter conditions.[8] For its part, the UNFCCC (2007) placed annual adaptation costs at $28 billion to $67 billion. The main increase in the World Bank study was in costs of coastal defense.

It is beyond the scope of the present study to evaluate these two main adaptation cost studies. However, certain questions warrant highlighting. First, the time-gradient of the costs is surprisingly low. The (NCAR scenario) averages are $72 billion for 2010–19, $89 billion for 2020–29, and $103 billion for 2030–49 (World Bank 2010b, 6). Damage functions for global warming are typically strongly nonlinear, so it would have been expected instead that the early adaptation costs would be more modest relative to those at mid-century. Although the report notes this implicit paradox "suggesting that countries become less vulnerable to climate change as their economies grow" (p. 4), its category estimates do not support this interpretation. For example, its coastal defense costs, which would be expected to grow more than linearly over time, do not do so (p. 44); and its health adaptation costs (for example, for defense against malaria), which would be expected to be the most amenable to reduction through economic development, are only a tiny part of the adaptation total ($2 billion annually; p. 7). It seems likely, then, that the annual costs

---

8. Curiously, the adaptation costs in agriculture did not turn out higher in the drier model than in the wetter model even in Africa and Latin America, areas with high agricultural vulnerability to global warming (Cline 2007), raising the question of whether the methodology is adequate.

may be overstated in the early decades relative to the costs estimated for the later decades.

Second, the report goes astray when it includes $7 billion in annual costs of educating women as its substitute for any concrete estimate concerning extreme weather events. This complete non sequitor unfortunately raises the question of whether political correctness is guiding calculations in the other categories.

For the question of international finance, however, there is a more fundamental question. What portion of the aggregate adaptation costs would it make sense to consider eligible for international support? Much of the infrastructure costs, as well as costs in other categories, will be in emerging-market economies that are not particularly likely to need external finance and are already at income levels well above eligibility for concessional assistance from such entities as the International Development Association (the concessional aid branch of the World Bank).

These considerations suggest that the World Bank and UNFCCC numbers for adaptation costs might reasonably be scaled back to some $50 billion per year in 2020 (tilting the time curve down toward the front and up toward the back, and considering that the UNFCCC estimates are lower than those of the World Bank). Further, if just China, Korea, Malaysia, and Taiwan are removed from the total as being either too rich by 2020 or too abundant in foreign exchange reserves to need external financing, and using GDP share in the absence of any country detail in the World Bank study, then by 2020 at least one-third of the total adaptation costs of developing countries would not be eligible for external finance. On this basis, appropriate interpretation of the World Bank and UNFCCC adaptation cost estimates might translate into a total of about $33 billion annually by 2020 that might be eligible for external finance. An alternative approach to the same question is to focus on the share of the two poorest regions in the total. For 2020–29, sub-Saharan Africa accounts for $17 billion in annual adaptation costs and South Asia $12 billion (World Bank 2010b, 6), which also turns out to sum to about $30 billion annually.

8

Synthesis

The findings of this study can be summarized in two broad categories: (1) abatement costs for a Copenhagen Accord path that is approximately consistent by 2050 with 450 parts per million (ppm) stabilization of carbon dioxide-equivalent atmospheric concentration and (2) implications for international financing for developing countries.[1] A summary range for global abatement costs is about one-fourth to two-thirds of 1 percent of GDP by 2030 and 1 to 2 percent by 2050, with the costs broadly similar for both industrial and developing countries. Financing to cover not only abatement investments but also adaptation costs for developing countries (but excluding China, and for adaptation also excluding Korea, Malaysia, and Taiwan) amounts to about $80 billion for 2020 and $170 billion for 2030. The notional $100 billion financing commitment in the Copenhagen Accord would thus be in the right order of magnitude for 2020, with some room to add in offset purchases. The implied financing figure could be twice as high by 2030.

The $100 Billion Copenhagen Commitment

To place the issue of international financing of action on climate change into a policy context, it is useful to emphasize that the Copenhagen Accord (UNFCCC 2010a) included the following text on financing from industrial countries:

> The collective commitment by developed countries is to provide new and additional resources, including forestry and investments through interna-

---

1. As noted earlier, the central Copenhagen Convergence scenario in this study limits 2050 atmospheric concentrations to estimated levels of 437 ppm for CO_2 itself and 476 ppm for CO_2-e including other greenhouse gases and aerosols.

tional institutions, approaching USD30 billion for the period 2010-2012 with balanced allocation between adaptation and mitigation. Funding for adaptation will be prioritized for the most vulnerable developing countries, such as the least developed countries, small island developing States and Africa. In the context of meaningful mitigation actions and transparency on implementation, developed countries commit to a goal of mobilizing jointly USD100 billion dollars a year by 2020 to address the needs of developing countries. This funding will come from a wide variety of sources, public and private, bilateral and multilateral.

The Cancún Agreements ratified the $100 billion financing target from Copenhagen. The origins of the $100 billion target for 2020 appear to have been primarily political rather than technical studies of abatement or adaptation costs. In mid-2009, then UK prime minister Gordon Brown called for $100 billion in funding annually from developed to developing countries by 2020 to combat climate change.[2] In October the European Union agreed that the global cost for addressing global warming would reach €100 billion annually by 2020, with up to half coming from public sources in the developed world. Trevor Houser (2010a, 10) notes that in the Copenhagen negotiations on December 16, 2009, the head of the G-77, Ethiopian president Meles Zenawi, announced that $100 billion per year in financial support by 2020 would be a sufficient offer from the developed countries. Houser also notes that this figure was considerably lower than previous G-77 requests that had ranged from $200 billion to $500 billion.

On December 17, 2009, US Secretary of State Hillary Clinton announced that "the United States is prepared to work with other counties toward a goal of jointly mobilizing $100 billion a year by 2020 to address the climate change needs of developing countries."[3] She conditioned this commitment as being "in the context of a strong accord in which all major economies stand behind meaningful mitigation actions...." She added that "We expect this funding will come from a wide variety of sources, public and private, bilateral and multilateral, including alternative sources of finance. This will include a significant focus on forestry and adaptation, particularly...for the poorest and most vulnerable among us." This endorsement of a specific $100 billion figure was an important element in making it possible to arrive at the Accord.

Three components of the 2020 financing are explicitly or implicitly present: investment in carbon abatement (e.g., renewable energy sources); adaptation expenses (e.g., seawalls); and purchase of carbon offsets. The first two categories are explicit in the Accord's phrase "balanced allocation between mitigation and adaptation," although that language is adjacent to the discussion of financing for 2010–12. The third component, offset purchases, is

2. "Rich must pay $100 bln yearly on climate—UK's Brown," Reuters, June 26, 2009.

3. Hillary Rodham Clinton, remarks at the United Nations Framework Convention on Climate Change, December 17, 2009, US Department of State, Washington, available at www.state.gov.

implicit in the language "public and private." The principal form in which private financing would enter climate change finance is purchases of offsets in developing countries by entities in industrial countries seeking to fulfill part of their abatement requirements.[4]

By late 2010 a high-level advisory group to UN Secretary-General Ban Ki-moon issued a report on prospective sources for the $100 billion financing target (United Nations 2010). The group judged that by 2020 a carbon price of $20 to $25 per ton of carbon dioxide could generate auction revenue of some $300 billion in industrial countries, of which 10 percent or $30 billion might reasonably be allocated to international financing. Such a price could also induce $100 billion to $200 billion in annual gross private investment flows, but the group was divided on whether such flows or only their "grant equivalent" should be included in the $100 billion target (and mentioned a notional $10 billion to $20 billion as the "net" flow in this concept). Additional amounts could include $10 billion annually from a carbon tax on international transportation, and $10 billion from redeployment of fossil fuel subsidies (or alternatively from a financial transactions tax). Annual international carbon market flows for offset purchases could reach $30 billion to $50 billion, but again the group was divided on whether these should count in the $100 billion target. Finally, the experts anticipated that net carbon-related flows from multilateral development banks could amount to $11 billion annually by 2020.

Estimates of This Study

Table 8.1 reports the central abatement cost estimates, based on the Copenhagen Convergence (CopCon) policy scenario applying the RICE model abatement cost functions and the EMF-alternative cost function. The final column reports the present value of abatement cost for the full period 2010–50, as a percent of the corresponding present value of GDP.

There are three central messages from table 8.1. First, the abatement costs to keep within the 450 ppm ceiling should be moderate, reaching about one-fourth to two-thirds of 1 percent of GDP by 2030 and about 1½ percent (industrial countries) or 1 percent of GDP (developing countries, RICE basis) to 2 percent (both industrial and developing, EMF-alternate basis) by 2050. Second, the costs can be reduced by international emissions trading, although by a considerably lesser proportion than is generally perceived. Thus, by 2040 the reduction would be only from 0.78 to 0.60 percent of GDP for industrial countries (RICE basis; not calculated for the EMF-alternate basis). Third, a more ambitious start on abatement could reduce the full-period costs. Reallocation of emissions cutbacks, primarily from 2040 to 2020, could reduce the present

---

4. As one observer noted at the time of Secretary Clinton's announcement, "a lot of this money could come, for example, from private sources, like carbon-offset projects purchased under domestic cap-and-trade programs." Brad Palmer, "A Closer Look at Clinton's $100 Billion Pledge," *New Republic*, December 17, 2009.

Table 8.1 Abatement costs for the Copenhagen Convergence (CopCon) policy path (percent of GDP)

Group	2020	2030	2040	2050	Present value, 2010–50[a]
		RICE cost basis			
CopCon					
Industrial	0.04	0.28	0.78	1.55	0.42
Developing	0.02	0.19	0.59	0.98	0.37
With trade					
Industrial	0.01	0.18	0.60	1.14	0.30
Developing	0.01	0.19	0.58	1.01	0.36
With reallocation					
Industrial	0.13	0.18	0.24	1.14	0.26
Developing	0.14	0.18	0.24	1.01	0.30
		EMF-alternate basis			
CopCon					
Industrial	0.23	0.67	1.29	2.09	0.74
Developing	0.07	0.62	1.41	2.02	0.88

a. Discounting at 3 percent.

Source: Author's calculations based on tables 5.4, 6.2, 6.3, and G.2.

value of abatement costs for the full period by about one-seventh for industrial countries (in comparison to the with-trade but fixed-decade targets) and about one-sixth for developing countries (RICE basis).

Table 8.2 presents parallel summary results for estimates of developing-country financing needs to cover abatement costs, adaptation costs, and implied financial flows for offset purchases. The estimates are for 2020 and 2030 only, for the purpose of remaining more closely within the time frame of the $100 billion benchmark cited in the Copenhagen Accord for 2020. Moreover, considering China's large foreign exchange reserves and unlikely need for recourse to external finance, the central estimate for abatement investment cost excludes China (although the nation is included in the alternative estimate in parentheses). Similarly, considering the prospectively relatively high levels of per capita income in Korea, Malaysia, and Taiwan, these three economies as well as China are excluded in the estimates of financing needs for adaptation.

For the first category, investment for abatement, the preferred estimates are discussed above. The main estimate excludes China on grounds that it is unlikely to need external finance; the amounts including China are shown in parentheses.

For adaptation costs, the discussion above suggests the need to impose a steeper gradient on the World Bank estimates. If the 2050 level is set at one-

Table 8.2   Developing-country financing needs for abatement and adaptation and financial flows from offset purchases
(billions of 2005 dollars)

	2020	2030
Investment for abatement[a]	41 (94)	118 (294)
Adaptation costs[b]	39	52
Offset purchases[c]	6 (29)	39
Total	86 (162)	209 (385)
Percent of industrial-country GDP	0.18 (0.35)	0.35 (0.67)

a. Excludes China (figure in parentheses includes China).
b. Excludes China, Korea, Malaysia, and Taiwan.
c. Alternative $25/tCO$_2$ basis in parentheses.

Source: Author's calculations.

third above the four-decade average and the 2020 level is set at one-third below the average, then, applying the $87 billion annual average of the wet- and dry-model scenarios, the result is annual abatement costs of $59 billion in 2020 and $116 billion in 2050, with 2030 interpolated at $78 billion. Applying a fraction of two-thirds to the abatement cost total to take account of exclusion of China, Korea, Malaysia, and Taiwan, the result is adaptation costs of $39 billion in 2020 and $52 billion in 2030. The estimate is somewhat lower if the World Bank and earlier UNFCCC estimates are averaged (about $33 billion in 2020, as discussed in chapter 7).

For offset purchases, the carbon shadow price in table 6.2 can be multiplied by the amount of carbon emissions rights traded to obtain financial flows associated with carbon trade. The result is a flow of $6 billion in 2020 and $39 billion in 2030. The 2020 estimate is low because of the extremely low carbon shadow price ($4.8) when marginal costs are equated across all countries in that year. Table 8.2 includes an alternative variant in which the 2020 carbon trading price is arbitrarily set at $25 per ton of CO_2, a level more reflective of conditions that might be expected to prevail in some areas (especially the European Trading Scheme) in the face of more realistic inefficiencies in global carbon trading. In the variant (in parentheses) the 2020 trading flow amounts to $29 billion.

The sum of financing benchmarks for the three concepts amounts to $86 billion in 2020 ($162 billion including China in abatement investment and using the higher offset-purchase variant) and $209 billion in 2030 ($385 billion including China in abatement investment).[5] These magnitudes amount

---

5. It might be asked whether the 2020 finance figure is understated because countries likely to request mitigation finance include many that have not yet listed national actions in the Accord's Appendix II.

to 0.18 percent (or 0.35 percent including China) of industrial-country GDP in 2020 and 0.35 percent (or 0.67 percent including China) in 2030. The absolute magnitudes suggest that the $100 billion figure for 2020 noted in the Copenhagen Accord may be moderately on the high side but is in the right order of magnitude and considerably lower than could be expected by 2030.

Finally, it should be recognized that the analysis of abatement costs in 2020 would be understated to the extent that numerous countries that have not yet signed up to the Copenhagen Accord initiatives might do so, boosting total abatement costs. It is useful to consider these countries in four groups. In a first group, there are approximately 50 developing countries that have not yet entered Appendix II undertakings but have per capita emissions below the endpoint CopCon target of 1.43 tCO_2 per capita. Their total emissions in 2005 amounted to 627 $GtCO_2$, with the largest emitters among them being Pakistan (127 million tons), Nigeria (98 million tons), Vietnam (96 million tons), the Philippines (80 million tons), and Bangladesh (39 million tons).[6] The emissions of this group are so low that it would probably not be cost efficient to seek much abatement among them (except where deforestation emissions, not included in these estimates, are sizable). A second group of nonadherents to the Accord comprises about 40 middle- or low-income developing countries with per capita emissions greater than the 1.43-ton eventual target. Their total emissions amounted to about 1.2 $GtCO_2$ in 2005. The largest emitters among them are Turkey (238 million tons in 2005), Thailand (233 million tons), Egypt (165 million tons), Uzbekistan (112 million tons), and North Korea (77 million tons). A third group comprises just two economies: Taiwan (272 million tons) and Malaysia (155 million tons). Neither has adhered, but it seems unlikely that if either were to do so, it would undertake a deeper commitment than China (and India), and hence unlikely that the commitment would represent a cutback from the business as usual baseline. Although neither has yet adhered, both are relatively rich economies that should be doing so and on a basis that does not require external financing. The fourth group comprises 15 oil-producing nations, with aggregate emissions of 1.5 $GtCO_2$ in 2005, with the largest including Iran (437 million tons), Saudi Arabia (335 million tons), Venezuela (152 million tons), Iraq (98 million tons), Algeria (96 million tons), and Kuwait (77 million tons). It seems highly improbable that countries in this grouping will undertake abatement and more likely that many will oppose international abatement efforts on grounds of unfair consequences for oil exporters.[7]

In contrast to the non- or late-adhering countries, total emissions of Copenhagen-adhering Appendix I countries amount to 14.4 $GtCO_2$ (2005 data) and Appendix II countries, 9.3 $GtCO_2$. The set of relevant potential additional adherents for which abatement by 2020 might make sense and would not

<hr />

6. The estimates here are calculated from World Resources Institute (2010).

7. Even though, ironically, in the initial decades a price on carbon dioxide emissions might boost the demand for oil by inducing substitution away from more carbon-intensive coal.

likely be ruled out by policy stance would be group 2 just mentioned. Their emissions would represent an increase of just 5 percent in the prospective pool of adherents.[8] On this basis, the global abatement cost estimates for 2020 are unlikely to be understated by very much from the standpoint of countries that might join in the effort but have not yet subscribed to the Copenhagen Accord undertakings. Any understatement in investment costs would be even smaller, because the estimates of table 7.1 in the previous chapter are premised on comprehensive adherence to the CopCon abatement path for the decade 2020–30, regardless of the commitment so far expressed regarding 2020.

8. That is, $1.2 / (14.4 + 9.3)$.

Appendices

Appendix A
Data Sources and Further Statistical Tables

The emissions data in table 2.1 in chapter 2 are from CDIAC (2009). The data underlying calculation of the growth rates are from the US Census Bureau (2009) for population, Heston, Summers, and Aten (2009) for purchasing power parity (ppp) per capita GDP, and World Resources Institute (2009) for energy use.

The baseline projections through 2030 in table 2.2 and appendix tables A.1 through A.4 are based on EIA (2009). For countries not specifically shown in detail in the EIA projections, future emissions are based on 2006 emissions, multiplied by the relevant ratios of 2020 and 2030 estimates for relevant regions to the corresponding 2006 levels for each of the variables in question.

Global emissions by 2030 shown in table 2.2, at 41.4 $GtCO_2$, are slightly higher than in EIA (2009), which places them at 40.4 $GtCO_2$. For the 25 countries shown individually in table 2.2, the aggregate (36.5 $GtCO_2$) is calculated to be identical to that in EIA (2009). The additional 1 $GtCO_2$ in the projections here stems from a more realistic estimate for emissions for the large bloc of poor countries in "rest of world developing" (4.4 $GtCO_2$ for 3.3 billion people) than would be implied by the residual between the estimate for the 25 emitters and the EIA (2009) world total.

Table A.1 Population (millions)

Country/group	2007	2020	2030	2040	2050	Growth rate (percent) 2007–30	Growth rate (percent) 2030–50
Argentina	40	45	49	52	54	0.86	0.46
Australia	21	24	26	28	29	0.99	0.54
Brazil	194	223	240	253	261	0.93	0.41
Canada	33	36	39	40	41	0.69	0.32
China	1,322	1,431	1,462	1,455	1,424	0.44	−0.13
Egypt	76	96	111	125	138	1.67	1.08
European Union	491	494	488	477	459	−0.02	−0.30
India	1,124	1,326	1,461	1,572	1,657	1.14	0.63
Indonesia	235	268	289	305	313	0.90	0.40
Iran	65	74	79	81	81	0.79	0.19
Japan	127	122	114	104	94	−0.50	−0.96
Kazakhstan	15	16	16	16	15	0.19	−0.28
Malaysia	25	31	35	39	43	1.53	1.01
Mexico	109	125	135	143	148	0.95	0.45
Pakistan	169	204	231	256	276	1.36	0.89
Russia	141	132	124	117	109	−0.57	−0.64
Saudi Arabia	28	34	38	44	50	1.41	1.33
South Africa	48	49	49	49	49	0.04	0.06
South Korea	48	49	49	47	43	0.07	−0.61

Taiwan	23	23	23	22	20	0.02	−0.65
Thailand	65	70	71	71	70	0.40	−0.11
Turkey	75	87	94	99	101	0.98	0.37
Ukraine	46	43	39	37	34	−0.69	−0.81
United States	301	341	374	406	439	0.93	0.81
Venezuela	26	31	35	38	40	1.28	0.71
25 emitters	4,847	5,372	5,670	5,873	5,989	0.68	0.27
Rest of world industrial	42	48	52	53	53	0.92	0.18
Rest of world developing	1,726	2,179	2,546	2,913	3,275	1.69	1.26
World	6,615	7,600	8,268	8,840	9,317	0.97	0.60
Industrial	1,156	1,198	1,216	1,224	1,225	0.22	0.04
Developing	5,459	6,402	7,052	7,616	8,092	1.11	0.69

Source: US Census Bureau (2009); author's calculations.

Table A.2 Baseline per capita GDP (thousands of 2005 ppp dollars)

Country/region/group	1990	2006	2010	2020	2030	Growth rate (percent) 2006–20	Growth rate (percent) 2020–30
OECD							
OECD North America	26.4	35.0	35.3	42.7	51.3	1.4	1.8
United States	31.7	42.6	42.8	51.2	60.6	1.3	1.7
Canada	27.6	36.5	37.5	44.0	52.2	1.3	1.7
Mexico	10.0	12.9	13.5	17.9	23.7	2.3	2.8
OECD Europe	19.5	26.4	27.4	33.5	40.7	1.7	1.9
OECD Asia	21.8	28.2	29.9	36.2	42.4	1.8	1.6
Japan	26.0	31.0	32.1	37.1	40.4	1.3	0.9
South Korea	8.7	18.5	21.2	30.4	40.4	3.6	2.8
Australia/New Zealand	24.3	32.6	34.6	43.6	54.8	2.1	2.3
Total OECD	22.3	29.9	30.8	37.6	45.3	1.6	1.9
Non-OECD							
Non-OECD Europe and Eurasia	8.7	9.2	11.6	17.2	22.9	4.4	2.9
Russia	12.6	12.8	16.6	25.2	34.1	4.9	3.0
Other	5.8	6.7	8.1	11.9	15.9	4.1	2.9
Non-OECD Asia	1.6	3.9	4.9	8.2	11.8	5.3	3.7
China	1.1	4.6	6.4	11.9	18.2	6.9	4.2
India	1.2	2.3	2.9	4.7	6.6	5.0	3.4

Other non-OECD Asia	2.9	4.7	5.4	7.8	10.8	3.6	3.3
Middle East	7.8	10.4	11.7	14.2	17.4	2.2	2.0
Africa	2.2	2.5	2.8	3.4	3.9	2.4	1.3
Central and South America	6.3	8.2	9.3	12.0	15.3	2.7	2.5
Brazil	7.0	8.4	9.5	12.5	16.6	2.8	2.8
Other Central and South America	5.8	8.0	9.2	11.6	14.4	2.6	2.2
Total non-OECD	2.9	4.6	5.6	8.3	11.1	4.2	3.0
Total world	6.9	9.8	10.8	14.2	18.2	2.7	2.5

OECD = Organization for Economic Cooperation and Development; ppp = purchasing power parity

Source: EIA (2009); author's calculations.

Table A.3 Business as usual baseline CO_2 emissions per capita
(metric tons)

Country/group	1990	2007	2020	2030	Growth rate (percent) 2007–20	2020–30
Argentina	3.4	4.3	4.6	4.6	0.46	0.11
Australia	17.3	18.1	16.8	16.6	−0.61	−0.08
Brazil	1.4	1.8	2.3	2.7	1.81	1.52
Canada	16.2	16.1	16.5	16.9	0.20	0.22
China	2.1	5.0	6.7	8.1	2.23	1.98
Egypt	1.4	2.5	2.2	2.2	−1.14	−0.14
European Union	8.9	8.3	8.2	8.5	−0.01	0.27
India	0.8	1.4	1.6	1.7	0.88	0.74
Indonesia	0.8	1.8	1.8	2.2	0.01	2.12
Iran	4.0	7.3	8.4	9.3	1.10	1.03
Japan	9.5	9.7	10.4	10.6	0.53	0.17
Kazakhstan	15.9	12.8	14.1	14.8	0.78	0.46
Malaysia	3.2	10.0	8.7	10.1	−1.07	1.49
Mexico	4.5	4.1	3.8	4.2	−0.61	0.97
Pakistan	0.6	0.9	1.0	1.2	0.96	1.63
Russia	14.0	11.2	13.5	14.6	1.43	0.80
Saudi Arabia	13.4	15.3	15.1	15.6	−0.10	0.33
South Africa	8.7	9.0	10.8	12.2	1.41	1.22
South Korea	5.6	9.9	11.5	12.8	1.19	1.05
Taiwan	6.2	11.5	16.7	22.5	2.87	3.01
Thailand	1.7	4.7	5.6	7.2	1.23	2.63
Turkey	2.6	3.9	3.1	2.9	−1.67	−0.62
Ukraine	11.8	6.9	8.7	9.9	1.77	1.21
United States	19.5	19.3	17.1	16.7	−0.95	−0.20
Venezuela	6.3	5.9	6.5	6.4	0.83	−0.28
25 emitters	4.9	5.6	6.0	6.4	0.49	0.77
Rest of world industrial	9.5	12.5	10.7	10.5	−1.21	−0.19
Rest of world developing	1.7	1.1	1.6	1.7	2.97	0.86
World	4.1	4.5	4.7	5.0	0.46	0.57
Industrial	12.5	12.2	12.1	12.4	−0.08	0.23
Developing	2.0	2.8	3.4	3.7	1.36	1.09

Source: EIA (2009); author's calculations.

Table A.4   Business as usual baseline energy consumption (quadrillion BTU)

Country/region/group	1990	2006	2010	2020	2030	Growth rate (percent) 2006–20	Growth rate (percent) 2020–30
OECD							
OECD North America	100.7	121.3	121.1	130.3	141.7	0.51	0.84
United States	84.7	100	99.9	105.4	113.6	0.38	0.75
Canada	11	14	14.6	16.5	18.3	1.17	1.04
Mexico	5	7.4	6.6	8.3	9.9	0.82	1.76
OECD Europe	70	81.6	82.2	87.9	91.8	0.53	0.43
OECD Asia	27	38.7	39.5	43.1	44.6	0.77	0.34
Japan	18.7	22.8	21.9	23.4	23	0.19	-0.17
South Korea	3.8	9.4	11	12	13.2	1.74	0.95
Australia/New Zealand	4.5	6.5	6.7	7.7	8.4	1.21	0.87
Total OECD	197.7	241.7	242.8	261.3	278.2	0.56	0.63
Non-OECD							
Non-OECD Europe and Eurasia	67.3	50.7	54	60.3	63.3	1.24	0.49
Russia	39.4	30.4	32.2	36	37.7	1.21	0.46
Other	28	20.3	21.7	24.3	25.6	1.28	0.52
Non-OECD Asia	47.4	117.6	139.2	190.3	239.6	3.44	2.30
China	27	73.8	90.5	124	155.8	3.71	2.28
India	7.9	17.7	19.1	26.8	32.3	2.96	1.87

(continued on next page)

Table A.4 Business as usual baseline energy consumption (quadrillion BTU) *(continued)*

Country/region/group	1990	2006	2010	2020	2030	Growth rate (percent) 2006–20	Growth rate (percent) 2020–30
		Non-OECD					
Other non-OECD Asia	12.5	26.1	29.6	39.5	51.5	2.96	2.65
Middle East	11.2	23.8	27.7	32.2	37.7	2.16	1.58
Africa	9.5	14.5	16.2	19.1	21.8	1.97	1.32
Central and South America	14.5	24.2	28.3	32.5	37.7	2.11	1.48
Brazil	5.8	9.6	11.4	14.5	18	2.95	2.16
Other Central and South America	8.8	14.6	17	18	19.7	1.50	0.90
Total non-OECD	149.9	230.8	265.4	334.4	400.1	2.65	1.79
Total world	347.7	472.4	508.3	595.7	678.3	1.66	1.30

OECD = Organization for Economic Cooperation and Development; BTU = British thermal units

Source: EIA (2009).

Appendix B
Estimating Atmospheric CO$_2$ Concentrations under Alternative Emissions Paths

Alternative emissions scenarios developed in the Intergovernmental Panel on Climate Change (IPCC) Special Report on Emissions Scenarios or SRES (Naki-ćenović et al. 2000) were considered in the IPCC's Third Assessment Report (TAR), which reported the corresponding atmospheric concentrations (IPCC 2001, pp. 801, 807). These estimates can be used to estimate future atmospheric concentrations as a function of total cumulative emissions.

Eleven business as usual emissions scenarios were considered. Their cumulative totals from 2011 through 2050 ranged from a low of 378 billion tons of carbon (GtC) for scenario B1p to a high of 657 GtC in scenario A1F1. The corresponding increases in atmospheric concentration from 2010 to 2050 ranged from a low of 84 parts per million (ppm) to a high of 178 ppm, respectively.[1]

A rough rule of thumb is that about one-half of the amount of emissions remains in the atmosphere.[2] The rest is taken up into soil and the oceans. Limits on the pace of this uptake suggest that the atmospheric retention rate should be lower if emissions are cut substantially but higher if they continue on a rapidly upward path. A regression using the 11 IPCC scenarios as "obser-

---

1. The then-projected 2010 concentration level was an average of 390 ppm, almost exactly the actual outcome (389.8 ppm; NOAA 2011).

2. In 1994 atmospheric stock stood at 762 GtC (2,797 GtCO$_2$); see IPCC (2007a, 515). At that time atmospheric concentration was 359 ppm (NOAA 2011). In 2009 concentration was at 387 ppm, placing atmospheric stock at $(387/359) \times 762 = 821$ GtC (3,013 GtCO$_2$). Annual fossil fuel emissions rose from 6.4 GtC in the 1990s to 7.2 GtC in 2000–05, and land use emissions (mainly deforestation) accounted for an additional 1.6 GtC per year (IPCC 2007a, 2). Cumulative emissions in 1995–2009 were thus approximately 120 GtC. With the increase in atmospheric stock amounting to 59 GtC, the "atmospheric retention ratio" was approximately 50 percent.

**Figure B.1   Business as usual emissions and increased atmospheric
concentrations: SRES scenario estimates and regression
equation**

change in concentration (ppm)

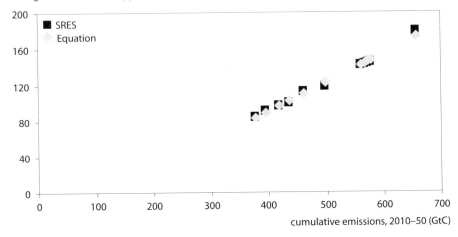

cumulative emissions, 2010–50 (GtC)

SRES = Intergovernmental Panel on Climate Change (IPCC) Special Report on Emissions Scenarios
ppm = parts per million
GtC = billion tons of carbon

Source: Author's calculations; see text.

vations" yields the following results for the 40-year increase in atmospheric
concentrations (2010 to 2050) as a function of cumulative emissions in this
same period:

$$\Delta C = -39.8 + 0.3236\ K;\ \mathrm{adj}\ R^2 = 0.992 \tag{B.1}$$
$$(8.4)\quad(34.6)$$

where ΔC is change in atmospheric concentration (ppm), K is cumulative emissions from 2010 to 2050 (GtC), and t-statistics are in parentheses. Figure B.1
shows the close adherence between the regression equation estimates and the
individual scenario projections.

The negative intercept indicates that if emissions ended immediately,
natural soil and ocean uptake would reduce concentrations by about 40 ppm
over the next four decades. At the margin, however, an extra billion tons of
carbon emitted raises atmospheric concentration by 0.32 ppm. This increment
amounts to 0.084 percent of concentration. Multiplying by the atmospheric
stock of 821 GtC, the atmospheric accumulation is 0.686 GtC. So although
the average retention ratio is only 50 percent, the marginal retention ratio is
about two-thirds.

The estimates of atmospheric concentrations in the main text apply equation B.1. For the decades ending 2020, 2030, and 2040, the intercept is set, respectively, at one-fourth, one-half, and three-fourths of the total-period intercept in the equation. Cumulative emissions through the period in question are used for the K term.

Appendix C
Other Greenhouse Gases
and Aerosols

This study focuses on emissions and concentrations of carbon dioxide. An important question is how much additional warming risk and abatement challenge is posed by other greenhouse gases. Correspondingly, if a target of stabilization at 450 parts per million (ppm) is set for total carbon dioxide–equivalent (CO_2-e) of all greenhouse gases, then the abatement challenge could be considerably more severe than that for stabilization at 450 ppm for carbon dioxide itself.

As in the case of identifying carbon dioxide concentrations under alternative emissions paths (appendix B), the Third Assessment Report of the Intergovernmental Panel on Climate Change (IPCC 2001) provides a basis for estimating a benchmark for the contribution of other greenhouse gases and aerosols (which I will call OGGA). The lowest-emission business as usual scenario in that report (B1p) would seem the best indication of OGGA effects under an international abatement strategy.[1] Table C.1 reports the radiative forcing of noncarbon greenhouse gases and aerosols as of 2050 in that scenario (IPCC 2001, 817–25).[2]

It is evident in the table that aerosols play an important role in moderating the influence of other greenhouse gases. In effect, aerosols act as a screen to deflect incoming solar radiation. The direct and indirect effects of aerosols sum to –1.13 watts per square meter (Wm^{-2}) (using B1p estimates for 2050 for direct effects and present-day levels for indirect cloud albedo effects).

---

1. In this scenario, "global population...peaks in mid-century and declines thereafter...[and there is] rapid change in economic structures toward a service and information economy, with reductions in material intensity and the introduction of clean and resource-efficient technologies...but without additional climate initiatives" (IPCC 2001, 63).

2. Radiative forcing is the anthropogenic increase in thermal energy in watts per square meter against the preindustrial 1750 base.

Table C.1 Radiative forcing of other greenhouse gases and aerosols by 2050 under business as usual low scenario B1p

Gas/aerosol	Radiative forcing (Wm⁻²)
Methane (CH$_4$)	0.58
Nitrous oxide (N$_2$O)	0.28
Tropospheric ozone (O$_3$)	0.52
Hydrofluorocarbons (HFCs)	0.096
Aerosols (direct)	
Sulphate (SO$_4$)	−0.3
Black carbon	0.37
Organic carbon	−0.45
Chlorofluorocarbons (CFCs) and hydrochlorofluorocarbons (HCFCs)	0.185
Indirect aerosol[a]	−0.75
Total	0.531

a. Cloud albedo effect from aerosols. Assumed constant at 2005 level.

Source: IPCC (2001, 817-25; 2007, 136).

Without their presence, the radiative effect from noncarbon greenhouse gases by 2050 would amount to an estimated 1.66 Wm⁻². Industrial aerosols, mainly sulphates, organic and black carbon, nitrates, and industrial dust, are concentrated over continental regions in the Northern Hemisphere. Unlike methane (CH$_4$), nitrous oxide (N$_2$O), and other "long-lived greenhouse gases" with atmospheric lifetimes of decades or centuries, aerosols have extremely short atmospheric residence of only a few days. Their ameliorating influence could thus be sharply reduced by mid-century if aggressive efforts to reduce industrial pollution greatly dominated the tendency for this pollution to rise as developing economies become more industrialized.[3]

Radiative forcing from carbon dioxide can be calculated as:

$$R = 6.3 \ln (C/280) \tag{C.1}$$

where R is radiative forcing in Wm⁻², C is atmospheric concentration of carbon dioxide in parts per million volume, and 280 is the preindustrial concentration level.[4] At benchmark doubling of preindustrial concentration, $C = 560$, and with $\ln (2) = 0.693$, $R = 4.4$ Wm⁻². Using the still central value for the climate

3. See IPCC (2007a, pp. 24, 29, 78).

4. Cline (1992, 21).

sensitivity parameter of equilibrium warming for doubling of carbon dioxide, 3°C, direct and indirect (after feedback) warming amounts to 0.682°C for each Wm⁻² radiative forcing (= $3°C/4.4Wm^{-2}$).

For 450 ppm concentration of CO_2, R = 2.99 Wm⁻². Multiplying by equilibrium warming per watt per square meter, 450 ppm translates to equilibrium warming of $2.99 \times 0.682 = 2.04°C$. It is on this basis that 450 ppm has been identified as the threshold of dangerous concentration associated with 2°C warming.

The additional warming to be expected from OGGA by 2050, based on table C.1 and the relationship of warming to radiative forcing, would amount to 0.36°C (= 0.531 Wm⁻² × 0.682). So as a first approximation, if carbon dioxide stabilizes at 450 ppm, then after taking account of the further warming influence of other greenhouse gases and the offsetting effect (and indirect effects) of likely aerosol concentrations, warming would amount to 2.36°C.

In broad terms, in this vicinity of warming the incorporation of OGGA increases the warming from CO_2 alone by 15 percent. It should be kept in mind, however, that this is just the central estimate, and warming could be somewhat lower or considerably higher. If one nonetheless considers it essential to focus on 450 ppm CO_2-e, then the necessary target for CO_2 alone will be lower.

Let C* be the target level of carbon dioxide concentration to yield CO_2-e = 450 ppm under the benchmark radiative forcing from OGGA estimated here, or R_O = 0.531 Wm⁻². Then:

$$6.3 \ln \left[\frac{C*}{280}\right] + 0.531 = 6.3 \ln \left[\frac{450}{280}\right] \qquad (C.2)$$

Solving,

$$C* = e^{\ln 450 - 0.531/6.3} = 413.6 \qquad (C.3)$$

So in view of the likely force of OGGAs as of 2050, a target of 450 ppm for CO_2-e would require a target of about 414 ppm for CO_2. The target range could then be considered as 414 ppm for CO_2 and 2°C, on the more stringent side, or 450 ppm for CO_2 and 2.36°C, on the less stringent side.

Similarly, if mid-century carbon dioxide concentrations are restrained to 450 ppm, one can calculate the corresponding total carbon dioxide equivalent concentration of CO_2 and OGGA as follows. Let K be the radiative forcing of 450 ppm carbon dioxide plus mid-century OGGA. This amount will equal 2.99 Wm⁻² plus 0.531 Wm⁻², as discussed above. Then defining total carbon dioxide equivalent concentration as C_e*, the level consistent with 450 ppm for carbon dioxide alone will be:

$$C_e^* = e^{\frac{K}{6.3} + \ln 280} = 489.6 \qquad (C.4)$$

Thus, if abatement efforts limit carbon dioxide concentration to 450 ppm by mid-century, total carbon-equivalent concentration including OGGA would amount to about 490 ppm.

Appendix D
Alternative Policy Paths for CO_2 Emissions, 2010–50

The emissions path for the central abatement scenario of this study, Copenhagen Convergence, is shown in table D.1. The path inferred from the United Nations Development Program (UNDP 2007) targets, as discussed in the main text, is shown in table D.2.

For the policy approach proposed by Chakravarty et al. (2009), shown in table D.3, the following procedure is used. That study reports total emissions and populations for 2003 and projections of 2030 populations, business as usual emissions, and policy-path emissions. For 10 countries in the present study there are country-specific projections.[1] For other countries, the paths shown in table D.3 are based on the paths for the country groupings in the Chakravarty et al. study that most closely map to the individual countries in the present study. From 2010 actual levels to 2030 policy path levels, the trajectories here apply a linear interpolation to estimate 2020 emissions.

Table D.4 reports the policy emissions paths implied by the Frankel (2008) study. Frankel reports per capita emissions data for 11 regions in five-year increments beginning in 2010.[2] Each of the 25 economies in the present study is mapped onto its corresponding region in the Frankel study. The Frankel projections are normalized to coincide with the 2010 Energy Information Administration (EIA) baseline estimates. For South Asia and sub-Saharan Africa, which do not face emissions caps until 2025 in the Frankel approach, emissions are assumed to follow the baseline paths identified in the present study until that year.

---

1. Australia–New Zealand, Brazil, Canada, China, India, Japan, Korea, Mexico, Russia, and the United States.

2. For China, the data in table D.4 are calculated from Frankel's total emissions divided by projected population, as the per capita emissions data indicated by Frankel are approximately one-third too low.

Table D.1 CO$_2$ emissions path under Copenhagen Convergence scenario (million tCO$_2$)

Country/group	2020	2030	2040	2050
Argentina	207	172	128	77
Australia	296	227	141	41
Brazil	389	394	389	373
Canada	465	347	209	59
China	9,544	7,197	4,622	2,037
Egypt	210	215	211	197
European Union	3,360	2,448	1,536	657
India	2,083	2,226	2,321	2,369
Indonesia	351	390	424	448
Iran	621	477	302	117
Japan	879	601	349	134
Kazakhstan	222	156	88	22
Malaysia	267	222	152	62
Mexico	330	303	263	212
Pakistan	203	264	329	395
Russia	1,660	1,098	599	156
Saudi Arabia	508	403	264	71
South Africa	345	255	163	71
South Korea	398	287	171	62
Taiwan	388	266	143	29
Thailand	388	299	201	100
Turkey	271	240	196	144
Ukraine	372	249	141	48
United States	4,848	3,714	2,307	628
Venezuela	205	169	119	58
25 emitters	28,811	22,618	15,765	8,564
Rest of world industrial	423	327	207	77
Rest of world developing	3,436	3,890	4,309	4,683
World	32,671	26,834	20,280	13,323
Industrial	11,932	8,762	5,347	1,752
Developing	20,739	18,072	14,934	11,571

Source: Author's calculations based on table 3.1 for 2020 and convergence thereafter; see text.

Table D.2 CO$_2$ emissions path under UNDP (2007) (million tCO$_2$)

Country/group	2020	2030	2040	2050
Argentina	207	168	137	90
Australia	205	150	110	59
Brazil	511	387	292	167
Canada	315	230	168	90
China	9,544	6,402	4,294	1,932
Egypt	210	154	113	61
European Union	2,940	2,149	1,571	840
India	2,083	1,495	1,073	553
Indonesia	475	337	239	120
Iran	621	457	336	182
Japan	821	600	439	234
Kazakhstan	225	221	217	209
Malaysia	267	172	110	45
Mexico	471	424	381	308
Pakistan	203	146	106	55
Russia	1,453	1,062	776	415
Saudi Arabia	508	387	296	172
South Africa	523	442	374	267
South Korea	569	434	332	193
Taiwan	388	277	198	101
Thailand	388	259	172	77
Turkey	271	220	178	117
Ukraine	372	398	427	489
United States	3,406	2,490	1,820	973
Venezuela	205	170	141	98
25 emitters	27,181	19,631	14,300	7,847
Rest of world industrial	210	154	112	60
Rest of world developing	3,436	3,491	3,547	3,602
World	30,827	23,277	17,959	11,509
Industrial	9,349	6,835	4,998	2,671
Developing	21,478	16,441	12,961	8,837

Source: UNDP (2007) and author's calculations (see chapter 5).

Table D.3 CO$_2$ emissions path under Chakravarty et al. (2009)
(million tCO$_2$)

Country/group	2020	2030
Argentina	215	228
Australia	318	265
Brazil	473	534
Canada	462	370
China	8,358	9,397
Egypt	188	192
European Union	3,671	3,377
India	2,074	2,552
Indonesia	399	424
Iran	439	337
Japan	1,152	1,092
Kazakhstan	203	199
Malaysia	237	264
Mexico	499	623
Pakistan	143	127
Russia	1,190	725
Saudi Arabia	424	406
South Africa	397	336
South Korea	511	471
Taiwan	291	276
Thailand	305	306
Turkey	323	382
Ukraine	341	340
United States	4,630	3,615
Venezuela	246	291
25 emitters	27,489	27,132
Rest of world industrial	490	485
Rest of world developing	3,436	4,374
World	31,415	31,991
Industrial	11,913	9,930
Developing	19,502	22,061

Source: Chakravarty et al. (2009) and author's calculations.

Table D.4 CO_2 emissions path under Frankel (2008) (million tCO_2)

Country/group	2020	2030	2040	2050
Argentina	294	392	488	444
Australia	329	268	205	140
Brazil	603	808	1,003	904
Canada	674	568	507	448
China	9,647	10,311	8,477	7,405
Egypt	197	182	169	154
European Union	3,453	2,763	2,093	1,418
India	2,083	2,733	3,817	5,094
Indonesia	488	521	430	376
Iran	532	452	383	321
Japan	1,312	974	766	595
Kazakhstan	140	108	77	47
Malaysia	293	334	291	271
Mexico	551	741	923	836
Pakistan	203	287	413	564
Russia	1,025	743	507	304
Saudi Arabia	452	412	392	368
South Africa	361	272	196	129
South Korea	446	332	228	137
Taiwan	366	358	266	209
Thailand	380	385	301	250
Turkey	192	160	122	80
Ukraine	209	150	101	59
United States	3,978	3,641	2,795	2,034
Venezuela	304	422	540	502
25 emitters	28,513	28,316	25,489	23,089
Rest of world industrial	542	505	415	337
Rest of world developing	3,436	4,374	5,416	6,549
World	32,491	33,194	31,320	29,975
Industrial	11,314	9,462	7,289	5,275
Developing	21,177	23,731	24,032	24,700

Source: Frankel (2008) and author's calculations.

Appendix E
Abatement Costs of the Alternative Policy Paths

Table E.1   Abatement costs: UNDP (2007) (percent of GDP)

Country/group	2020	2030	2040	2050
Argentina	0.00	0.07	0.26	0.67
Australia	0.64	1.18	1.47	1.83
Brazil	0.00	0.24	0.74	1.35
Canada	0.60	1.14	1.46	1.83
China	0.00	0.56	1.41	2.17
Egypt	0.00	0.18	0.56	1.10
European Union	0.09	0.36	0.63	1.08
India	0.00	0.39	1.12	2.01
Indonesia	0.00	0.68	1.79	2.75
Iran	0.00	0.28	0.87	1.69
Japan	0.25	0.55	0.79	1.30
Kazakhstan	0.00	0.00	0.01	0.01
Malaysia	0.00	0.90	2.17	3.09
Mexico	0.00	0.06	0.24	0.53
Pakistan	0.00	0.64	1.72	2.68
Russia	0.04	0.31	0.65	1.26
Saudi Arabia	0.00	0.24	0.82	1.62
South Africa	0.00	0.07	0.28	0.65
South Korea	0.00	0.14	0.46	1.05
Taiwan	0.00	0.66	1.74	2.69

(continued on next page)

Table E.1   Abatement costs: UNDP (2007) (percent of GDP)
(continued)

Country/group	2020	2030	2040	2050
Thailand	0.00	0.81	2.03	2.97
Turkey	0.00	0.03	0.12	0.39
Ukraine	0.00	0.00	0.00	0.00
United States	0.30	0.70	0.99	1.34
Venezuela	0.00	0.06	0.21	0.55
25 emitters	0.11	0.49	1.03	1.67
Rest of world industrial	1.10	1.52	1.67	1.90
Rest of world developing	0.00	0.05	0.18	0.31
World	0.11	0.42	0.84	1.32
Industrial	0.26	0.61	0.89	1.30
Developing	0.00	0.30	0.81	1.33

Source: Author's calculations based on RICE model (table 4.1) and table D.2.

Table E.2   Abatement costs: Chakravarty et al. (2009) (percent of GDP)

Country/group	2020	2030
Argentina	0.00	0.00
Australia	0.06	0.27
Brazil	0.00	0.02
Canada	0.08	0.37
China	0.02	0.06
Egypt	0.01	0.04
European Union	0.01	0.02
India	0.00	0.00
Indonesia	0.04	0.25
Iran	0.18	0.79
Japan	0.01	0.00
Kazakhstan	0.01	0.02
Malaysia	0.02	0.13
Mexico	0.00	0.00
Pakistan	0.23	0.97
Russia	0.20	0.87
Saudi Arabia	0.04	0.18
South Africa	0.08	0.32
South Korea	0.01	0.08
Taiwan	0.15	0.67
Thailand	0.09	0.46
Turkey	0.00	0.00
Ukraine	0.00	0.01
United States	0.04	0.26
Venezuela	0.00	0.00
25 emitters	0.03	0.15
Rest of world industrial	0.00	0.01
Rest of world developing	0.00	0.00
World	0.03	0.12
Industrial	0.04	0.19
Developing	0.02	0.07

Source: Author's calculations based on RICE model (table 4.1) and table D.3.

Table E.3   Abatement costs: Frankel (2008) (percent of GDP)

Country/group	2020	2030	2040	2050
Argentina	0.00	0.00	0.00	0.00
Australia	0.04	0.26	0.60	1.00
Brazil	0.00	0.00	0.00	0.00
Canada	0.00	0.01	0.08	0.18
China	0.00	0.02	0.32	0.63
Egypt	0.00	0.06	0.16	0.25
European Union	0.02	0.13	0.33	0.63
India	0.00	0.00	0.00	0.00
Indonesia	0.00	0.04	0.60	1.12
Iran	0.02	0.30	0.66	0.95
Japan	0.00	0.04	0.12	0.24
Kazakhstan	0.32	0.68	1.02	1.31
Malaysia	0.00	0.00	0.29	0.68
Mexico	0.00	0.00	0.00	0.00
Pakistan	0.00	0.00	0.00	0.00
Russia	0.40	0.83	1.23	1.54
Saudi Arabia	0.01	0.17	0.39	0.61
South Africa	0.16	0.59	1.01	1.28
South Korea	0.06	0.47	0.99	1.41
Taiwan	0.00	0.21	1.11	1.72
Thailand	0.00	0.12	0.88	1.47
Turkey	0.11	0.24	0.45	0.74
Ukraine	0.48	0.97	1.34	1.56
United States	0.14	0.25	0.53	0.79
Venezuela	0.00	0.00	0.00	0.00
25 emitters	0.06	0.14	0.37	0.61
Rest of world industrial	0.00	0.00	0.06	0.17
Rest of world developing	0.00	0.00	0.00	0.00
World	0.05	0.11	0.28	0.45
Industrial	0.09	0.21	0.45	0.72
Developing	0.01	0.05	0.19	0.33

Source: Author's calculations based on RICE model (table 4.1) and table D.4.

Appendix F
Cost-Minimizing Reallocation
of Abatement over Time

As discussed in the main text, the global minimum-cost abatement program consistent with meeting the cumulative emissions targets of the Copenhagen Convergence policy scenario can be calculated using a minimization algorithm.[1] Abatement cost is calculated using equation 4.1. Minimization of discounted present value will depend on the discount rate applied. Tables F.1 to F.3 apply 1.5, 3, and 5 percent per year, respectively, as alternatives. As I have argued in Cline (1992), for very long term issues such as climate change, the low end of this range is appropriate. However, inclusion of the higher rates provides information on the sensitivity of the outcome to the rate chosen. As discussed in the main text, the principal message of the various sets of results is that global abatement cost could be significantly reduced by adopting somewhat more aggressive abatement at the beginning of the period (2020), which given the constraints tends to have the effect of transferring some of the emissions otherwise incurred in 2020 to 2040 while leaving emissions in 2030 and in 2050 relatively unchanged.

---

1. The "Solver" routine in Microsoft Excel.

Table F.1 **Emissions profile under cost-minimization discounting at 1.5 percent per year** (million metric tons of CO_2 per year)

Country/group	2020	2030	2040	2050
Argentina	143	151	157	83
Australia	268	279	284	130
Brazil	388	469	553	378
Canada	403	410	406	120
China	6,208	7,283	8,297	2,728
Egypt	140	147	150	31
European Union	2,803	2,730	2,618	1,133
India	1,563	1,811	2,053	1,488
Indonesia	360	458	566	368
Iran	370	391	390	47
Japan	912	810	696	214
Kazakhstan	112	107	99	12
Malaysia	192	245	303	184
Mexico	346	401	453	295
Pakistan	159	205	258	208
Russia	1,047	1,010	975	167
Saudi Arabia	324	358	399	104
South Africa	230	183	103	38
South Korea	408	431	438	217
Taiwan	283	349	407	131
Thailand	268	329	386	81
Turkey	193	193	188	110
Ukraine	188	169	147	21
United States	3,740	3,806	3,833	1,190
Venezuela	125	132	135	48
25 emitters	21,173	22,857	24,295	9,527
Rest of world industrial	384	388	377	205
Rest of world developing	2,743	3,418	4,150	3,591
World	24,299	26,663	28,822	13,323
Industrial	9,557	9,433	9,190	3,159
Developing	14,743	17,230	19,632	10,164
Shadow price (dollars per ton)	47.1	54.7	63.5	217.5

Source: Author's calculations based on RICE model (table 4.1).

Table F.2   Emissions profile under cost-minimization discounting at 3 percent per year (million metric tons of CO_2 per year)

Country/group	2020	2030	2040	2050
Argentina	149	152	151	83
Australia	280	281	272	130
Brazil	399	472	537	378
Canada	421	414	386	120
China	6,512	7,351	7,871	2,728
Egypt	146	149	142	31
European Union	2,918	2,750	2,513	1,133
India	1,610	1,820	1,997	1,488
Indonesia	371	460	548	368
Iran	393	396	360	47
Japan	944	815	667	214
Kazakhstan	123	108	89	12
Malaysia	198	246	292	184
Mexico	357	403	439	295
Pakistan	163	206	252	208
Russia	1,114	1,022	915	167
Saudi Arabia	341	361	377	104
South Africa	257	189	64	38
South Korea	423	434	422	217
Taiwan	293	352	389	131
Thailand	279	331	366	81
Turkey	200	194	182	110
Ukraine	204	173	129	21
United States	3,931	3,840	3,637	1,190
Venezuela	132	133	128	48
25 emitters	22,160	23,052	23,122	9,527
Rest of world industrial	396	390	365	205
Rest of world developing	2,806	3,432	4,062	3,591
World	25,362	26,874	27,549	13,323
Industrial	10,005	9,512	8,755	3,159
Developing	15,357	17,362	18,794	10,164
Shadow price (dollars per ton)	39.7	53.3	71.7	217.5

Source: Author's calculations based on RICE model (table 4.1).

Table F.3 Emissions profile under cost-minimization discounting at 5 percent per year (million metric tons of CO_2 per year)

Country/group	2020	2030	2040	2050
Argentina	156	154	143	83
Australia	295	285	257	130
Brazil	413	476	515	378
Canada	443	419	360	120
China	6,886	7,459	7,312	2,728
Egypt	154	151	131	31
European Union	3,060	2,783	2,373	1,133
India	1,668	1,836	1,922	1,488
Indonesia	383	465	524	368
Iran	421	404	319	47
Japan	984	825	628	214
Kazakhstan	135	111	75	12
Malaysia	207	249	277	184
Mexico	371	407	420	295
Pakistan	168	208	243	208
Russia	1,197	1,041	835	167
Saudi Arabia	361	367	348	104
South Africa	290	199	34	38
South Korea	441	438	401	217
Taiwan	305	356	366	131
Thailand	292	336	339	81
Turkey	208	196	174	110
Ukraine	225	178	106	21
United States	4,163	3,899	3,379	1,190
Venezuela	141	135	119	48
25 emitters	23,370	23,376	21,602	9,527
Rest of world industrial	410	393	350	205
Rest of world developing	2,884	3,454	3,946	3,591
World	26,664	27,224	25,897	13,323
Industrial	10,553	9,645	8,181	3,159
Developing	16,111	17,578	17,716	10,164
Shadow price (dollars per ton)	31.3	51.0	83.1	217.5

Source: Author's calculations based on RICE model (table 4.1).

Appendix G
Abatement Cost Function
Estimates Based on EMF 22

As indicated in the main text, the functional form applied for the main estimates of this study treats abatement cost, as a fraction k of GDP, as being equal to a coefficient α multiplied by the proportionate cutback in emissions from their baseline level, μ, raised to an exponent β. Thus:

$$k = \alpha\mu^{\beta} \tag{G.1}$$

This form is adopted from the DICE (global) and RICE (regionally specific) models of Nordhaus (2008, 2010a, 2010b).

Over the past several years the Energy Modeling Forum (EMF) of Stanford University has carried out successive rounds of climate change policy analyses based on simulations of a number of the leading Integrated Assessment Models. In its most recent round, EMF 22, 11 models were applied to examine the economic and energy aspects of meeting alternative abatement targets under alternative scenarios for the timing of action.[1] Given the alternative scenarios, and in some cases alternative variants of the model in question, there were typically three to eight time-path estimates of abatement and corresponding abatement costs for each model, for each region. The regions were the United States, the European Union, China, India, "Group 1" comprising Annex I countries excluding Russia, "Group 2" comprising the BRICs (Brazil,

---

1. The targets were stabilization at 450, 550, or 650 parts per million (ppm) CO_2-equivalent. The scenarios were "full" for immediate full participation and "delayed" for no action by non-Annex I countries and Russia until 2030. Two variants of the targets were included: "never to exceed" and "overshoot," with the latter allowing temporary overshooting of the target concentration but with a return to the target level by 2100. See Clarke, Edmonds, Krey, Richels, Rose, and Tavoni (2009) and Fawcett et al. (2009).

Russia, India, and China), and "Group 3" comprising other emerging-market and developing countries. The EMF 22 compilation reported each model's reference baseline emissions and GDP paths, and for each scenario adjusted emissions and adjusted GDP after taking account of abatement costs.[2] The estimates are for 2010, 2020, 2030, 2040, and 2050.

Because each model run generates a proportionate cut from the (model's) baseline and a corresponding proportionate change in GDP, these results as a group may be seen as a sample of observations on abatement costs that can serve as the data input for synthesizing cost functions. The present study uses simple regression analysis to estimate equation G.1 using the EMF 22 "sample." The regression equation is obtained by taking the natural logarithm of both sides of equation G.1 to obtain:

$$\ln k = \ln \alpha + \beta \ln \mu = a + b \ln \mu; \ \alpha = e^a, \ \beta = b \tag{G.2}$$

Table G.1 reports the results of estimating regression equation G.2 for each of the regions in the EMF 22 model result compilation. In each case, the observations for 2020 were pooled with those of 2030 to estimate one equation and the observations for 2040 pooled with those for 2050 to estimate a second equation. In each case a dummy variable was added for the second of the two decades, but in most cases it was found not to be statistically significant. Where the dummy variable is significant, there are two reported values for α: one for the first of the two decades in question; the second, for the second decade. In all regressions, observations with cuts from baseline by less than 5 percent or more than 95 percent were excluded as not relevant for policy purposes. Moreover, inclusion of cuts near zero causes severe distortions because of the logarithmic formulation.[3]

An important feature of the EMF-based results is that the cost functions have much milder nonlinearity than those in the RICE model. Thus, the exponent β in the cost function is uniformly 2.8 in the RICE model. In contrast, there is some variation in the estimates from the EMF compilation, from a minimum of 1.16 (United States, 2040–50) to a maximum of 1.76 (Group 3, 2040–50). The average β from the EMF-based estimates is 1.46, only about half the value used in the RICE model. The practical effect of the higher nonlinearity in the RICE cost function is that although it arrives at relatively comparable abatement cost estimates by late in the period when cuts from baseline are deep, it yields far lower abatement costs early in the horizon when cuts are shallow. The lower costs at low cutbacks follow from the fact that costs are more comparable for deep cutbacks, combined with greater nonlinearity.

---

2. The detailed compilations are available for the United States at: http://emf.stanford.edu/files/evnts/5613/EMF_22_USA_Data_Update_2009-09-10.xls; and for other regions at: http://emf.stanford.edu/files/evnts/5613/EMF_22_International_Data_Update_2009-10-22.xls (the latter is referred to below as "EMF-International").

3. Because the logarithm approaches negative infinity as the cut approaches zero.

As discussed in the main text, the abatement cost equations estimated using the EMF 22 data tend to give surprisingly high costs for developing countries, especially in the later periods. Another part of the EMF exercise was to estimate global carbon prices under alternative scenarios. For the scenarios seeking a 450 ppm objective, the median model estimate of the global price for carbon dioxide was as follows: $77 per ton in 2020, $91 in 2030, $149 in 2040, and $228 in 2050.[4] In contrast, the estimated cost functions in combination with the Copenhagen Convergence (CopCon) abatement scenario generate marginal costs that reach far higher, for example, $570 per ton of CO_2 for Brazil in 2040 (table 6.1 in chapter 6).

As an alternative EMF-based cost estimate, then, it is assumed that the emissions cuts occur domestically for that part of the cost curve that has marginal cost below the global carbon price and that the rest of the target cut can be carried out at the global carbon price. In figure G.1, the country's marginal cost under CopCon for the year in question is "x." A linearized approximation of its domestic cost curve is the straight line between the origin and "x"; actual domestic cost would be somewhat lower because of nonlinearity. Achieving the emissions cut solely at home would have a total cost of the areas of triangles A, B, and C. If instead emissions rights can be purchased at the international carbon price of P_c, then only the cutbacks carried out at home have a cost based on the domestic cost curve. These cuts will be up to the amount R_h, where R refers to absolute emissions reductions (million tons) and subscript "h" indicates the amount carried out at home. The rest of the "cuts" are obtained through emissions rights purchases at the global carbon price. The fraction of the total cut R_T that will be carried out at home will be: $\phi_h = P_c/MC^*$, where MC^* is the marginal cost of the domestic cost curve at the full amount of the abatement R_T.

The alternate abatement cost estimate is then: $C' = R_T [\phi_h(P_c/2)+(1-\phi_h) P_c]$. The first part of the expression in brackets represents the average price in triangle A, which is one-half the international carbon price. The total abatement cost is then the area of triangle A plus rectangle B and is smaller than the cost estimated with the domestic cost equation by the amount of triangle C.

Table 5.5 in chapter 5 reports the unconstrained abatement cost estimates using the EMF-based cost functions of table 4.2 in chapter 4 and table G.1. Table G.2 reports the corresponding constrained abatement cost estimates obtained when the global carbon price is imposed as the ceiling for marginal cost in each country, as just discussed.

Finally, the main text sets forth a method for calculating investment cost associated with a given estimate for abatement cost. Table 7.1 in chapter 7 reports the resulting investment estimates for the EMF-based cost functions and CopCon abatement, expressed as percentages of GDP. Table G.3 reports the same cost estimates for 2020 and 2030 in terms of billions of 2005 purchasing power parity (ppp) dollars.

---

4. EMF-International, 2010.

Table G.1 Regression results for abatement cost function (t-statistics in parentheses)

Region	Period	Observations	a	b (=β)	D	Adjusted R²	α (=eᵃ)
United States	2020–30	128	−3.021 (−17.0)	1.569 15.7	...	0.67	0.049
	2040–50	129	−3.772 (−26.6)	1.158 8.5	...	0.36	0.023
European Union	2020–30	83	−3.684 (−19.0)	1.278 11.9	...	0.63	0.025
	2040–50	92	−3.719 (−34.9)	1.442 14.5	...	0.69	0.024
China	2020–30	54	−2.438 (−12.8)	1.381 11.5	...	0.71	0.087
	2040–50	92	−2.308 (−16.7)	1.586 14.3	−0.250 (−1.97)	0.70	0.0995; 0.0775
India	2020–30	48	−2.409 (−14.7)	1.545 14.8	...	0.82	0.090
	2040–50	71	−2.715 (−22.5)	1.412 10.9	...	0.63	0.066
Group 1	2020–30	90	−3.463 (−18.6)	1.457 14.1	...	0.69	0.031
	2040–50	92	−3.517 (−20.0)	1.612 11.0	−0.348 (−2.28)	0.57	0.0297; 0.0210

(continued on next page)

Group 2						
	2020–30	55	−2.292 (−11.6)	1.532 −12.1	⋯	0.73	0.101
	2040–50	92	−2.62 (−23.7)	1.336 −12.1	⋯	0.61	0.073
Group 3						
	2020–30	50	−2.381 (−8.4)	1.413 −8.9	⋯	0.62	0.092
	2040–50	60	−2.279 (−10.3)	1.764 −10.8	−0.387 (−2.1)	0.66	0.1024; 0.0696

Source: Author's statistical tests based on EMF 22 model results compilation; see text.

Figure G.1 Abatement cost with purchases of emissions rights

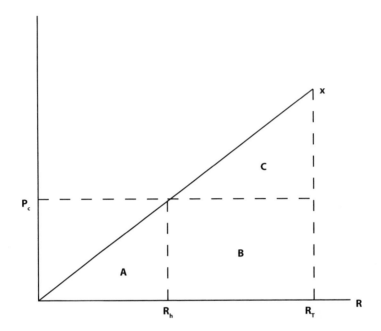

Note: See text for explanation of figure.

Table G.2 Abatement costs for the Copenhagen Convergence policy path: EMF 22 synthesis model basis constrained

Country/group	Percent of GDP				Amount (billions of 2005 ppp dollars)			
	2020	2030	2040	2050	2020	2030	2040	2050
Argentina	0.00	0.41	1.09	1.90	0	4	15	33
Australia	0.44	0.76	1.32	1.81	5	11	25	45
Brazil	0.30	0.50	0.89	1.37	9	21	52	109
Canada	0.36	0.75	1.66	1.83	6	15	40	54
China	0.00	1.22	2.86	4.11	0	323	1,150	2,471
Egypt	0.00	0.20	0.52	0.91	0	2	5	12
European Union	0.17	0.48	0.89	1.89	29	96	211	523
India	0.00	0.16	0.37	0.62	0	16	56	140
Indonesia	0.54	0.85	1.52	2.01	8	19	49	93
Iran	0.00	1.25	3.44	4.84	0	16	55	95
Japan	0.39	0.76	1.30	1.67	18	35	60	75
Kazakhstan	0.02	1.30	3.42	5.00	0	5	16	30
Malaysia	0.00	1.01	2.51	3.84	0	10	38	89
Mexico	0.44	0.67	1.19	1.69	10	22	54	105
Pakistan	0.00	0.03	0.09	0.16	0	0	2	4
Russia	0.17	1.22	2.42	3.84	6	52	130	261
Saudi Arabia	0.00	0.98	2.72	4.50	0	13	52	119
South Africa	1.37	2.79	5.46	5.87	8	19	43	53

(continued on next page)

127

Table G.2   Abatement costs for the Copenhagen Convergence policy path: EMF 22 synthesis model basis constrained (*continued*)

Country/group	Percent of GDP				Amount (billions of 2005 ppp dollars)			
	2020	2030	2040	2050	2020	2030	2040	2050
South Korea	0.58	1.07	2.03	2.94	11	27	66	117
Taiwan	0.00	1.39	3.57	5.23	0	19	64	119
Thailand	0.00	1.38	3.52	4.82	0	15	54	99
Turkey	0.00	0.11	0.30	0.57	0	2	6	15
Ukraine	0.00	0.71	1.49	1.73	0	4	10	15
United States	0.23	0.73	1.40	2.07	40	167	410	774
Venezuela	0.00	0.57	1.54	2.68	0	4	14	32
25 emitters	0.17	0.78	1.71	2.60	148	914	2,677	5,484
Rest of world industrial	0.18	0.51	1.03	1.64	4	13	33	61
Rest of world developing	0.00	0.12	0.29	0.46	0	39	139	333
World	0.14	0.64	1.37	2.05	152	966	2,849	5,878
Industrial	0.23	0.67	1.29	2.09	106	388	909	1,794
Developing	0.07	0.62	1.41	2.02	46	578	1,940	4,083

Source: Author's calculations; see text.

Table G.3 Investment required for Copenhagen Convergence abatement: 2020 and 2030
(billions of 2005 ppp dollars)

Country/group	2020				2030		
	McKinsey	RICE	EMF	EMF-alternate	RICE	EMF	EMF-alternate
Argentina	0.0	0.2	3.4	1.2	1.1	8.1	3.4
Australia	0.8	1.7	3.3	2.1	4.8	6.0	5.1
Brazil	0.8	2.1	20.1	4.0	4.7	28.7	10.3
Canada	1.4	2.4	4.9	3.3	6.7	8.5	9.3
China	8.0	24.2	163.2	82.5	115.9	437.6	235.4
Egypt	0.0	0.0	0.8	0.5	0.1	1.4	1.2
European Union	6.6	12.8	40.0	23.7	39.0	63.2	48.0
India	0.1	0.2	6.5	4.1	1.4	19.9	11.6
Indonesia	0.3	1.8	9.9	3.4	3.7	14.7	9.4
Iran	0.5	0.8	7.4	4.5	4.3	16.9	13.2
Japan	2.1	7.1	13.6	8.9	13.5	17.6	15.0
Kazakhstan	0.1	0.2	2.0	1.3	1.0	4.9	3.8
Malaysia	0.2	0.9	5.9	2.5	5.3	15.3	7.9
Mexico	0.5	2.6	19.8	4.0	5.8	32.9	10.6
Pakistan	0.0	0.0	0.2	0.1	0.0	0.3	0.3
Russia	0.8	3.2	28.5	13.8	13.5	49.3	28.7
Saudi Arabia	0.3	0.7	7.0	3.6	4.8	18.7	11.7

(continued on next page)

Table G.3 Investment required for Copenhagen Convergence abatement: 2020 and 2030 (billions of 2005 ppp dollars) *(continued)*

Country/group	2020 McKinsey	2020 RICE	2020 EMF	2020 EMF-alternate	2030 RICE	2030 EMF	2030 EMF-alternate
South Africa	1.9	1.2	6.9	4.6	2.2	10.7	10.1
South Korea	0.6	4.5	22.4	5.8	10.0	40.1	14.4
Taiwan	0.8	2.8	12.3	5.1	10.1	25.7	14.6
Thailand	0.5	1.5	8.0	4.1	6.2	17.4	11.9
Turkey	0.0	0.0	0.7	0.5	0.4	1.8	1.5
Ukraine	0.2	0.4	1.2	1.2	1.6	2.4	2.4
United States	4.4	14.2	67.0	40.3	52.1	72.1	88.7
Venezuela	0.0	0.1	2.3	1.0	0.9	6.0	3.2
25 emitters	30.9	85.6	457.2	225.9	308.9	920.3	571.7
Rest of world industrial	0.6	2.1	5.3	3.2	6.7	9.6	7.5
Rest of world developing	0.0	0.7	32.7	9.8	4.5	51.9	28.2
World	31.6	88.4	495.3	239.0	320.1	981.7	607.4
Industrial	16.7	43.4	162.6	95.4	136.3	226.4	202.4
Developing	14.9	45.0	332.7	143.6	183.8	755.3	405.0

Source: Author's calculations based on tables 5.4, 5.5, 5.6, and G.2.

References

Ackerman, Frank, Elizabeth Stanton, and Ramon Bueno. 2010. *CRED: A New Model of Climate and Development*. Stockholm Environment Institute Working Paper WP-US-10-03 (April). Somerville, MA: Stockholm Environment Institute. Available at www.sei-us.org.

CBO (Congressional Budget Office). 2009. *The Costs of Reducing Greenhouse-Gas Emissions*. Washington (November).

CDIAC (Carbon Dioxide Information Analysis Center). 2009. *Global, Regional, and National Fossil-Fuel CO_2 Emissions*. Oak Ridge, TN: Oak Ridge National Laboratory, US Department of Energy.

Chakravarty, Shoibal, Ananth Chikkatur, Heleen de Coninck, Stephen Pacala, Robert Socolow, and Massimo Tavoni. 2009. Sharing Global CO_2 Emission Reductions among One Billion High Emitters. *Proceedings of the National Academy of Sciences, PNAS Early Edition*. Washington. Available at www.pnas.org.

Clarke, L., C. Böhringer, and T. F. Rutherford. 2009. International, US, and EU Climate Change Control Scenarios: Results from EMF 22. *Energy Economics* 31, supplement 2: S63–S306.

Clarke, Leon, Jae Edmonds, Volker Krey, Richard Richels, Steven Rose, and Massimo Tavoni. 2009. International Climate Policy Architectures: Overview of the EMF 22 International Scenarios. *Energy Economics* 31: S64–S81.

Cline, William R. 1992. *The Economics of Global Warming*. Washington: Institute for International Economics.

Cline, William R. 2007. *Global Warming and Agriculture: Impact Estimates by Country*. Washington: Center for Global Development and Peterson Institute for International Economics.

Cline, William R. 2010a. Economic Analysis and Climate Change Policy: An Editorial Comment. *Climatic Change* 101, no. 3: 387–93.

Cline, William R. 2010b. US Climate Change Policy: Implementing Copenhagen and Beyond. Paper presented at conference on the Transatlantic Relationship in an Era of Growing Multipolarity, Washington, Peterson Institute for International Economics, October 8. Available at www.piie.com.

Cline, William R. 2011. Valuation of Damages from Climate Change. Speech presented at conference on Improving the Assessment and Valuation of Climate Change Impacts for Policy and Regulatory Analysis, Environmental Protection Agency and US Department of Energy, Washington, January 27–28. Available at www.piie.com.

Creyts, Jon, Anton Derkach, Scott Nyquist, Ken Ostrowski, and Jack Stephenson. 2007. *Reducing U.S. Greenhouse Gas Emissions: How Much at What Cost?* New York: McKinsey & Company.

EIA (Energy Information Administration). 2009. *International Energy Outlook 2009.* Report DOE/EIA-0484. Washington: Department of Energy.

ERI (China Energy Research Institute). 2009. *2050 China Energy and CO2 Emissions Report.* Beijing: Science Press.

Fawcett, Allen A., Katherine V. Calvin, Francisco C. de la Chesnaye, John M. Reilly, and John P. Weyant. 2009. Overview of EMF 22 US Transition Scenarios. *Energy Economics* 31: S198–S211.

Frankel, Jeffrey. 2008. *An Elaborated Proposal for a Global Climate Policy Architecture: Specific Formulas and Emission Targets for All Countries in All Decades.* Discussion Paper 08-08 (October). Cambridge, MA: Harvard Project on International Climate Agreements, Belfer Center for Science and International Affairs, Harvard Kennedy School.

Govtrack. 2009. *H. R. 2454: American Clean Energy and Security Act of 2009.* Available at www.govtrack.us.

Heston, Alan, Robert Summers, and Betina Aten. 2009. *Penn World Table Version 6.3.* Center for International Comparisons of Production, Income, and Prices (August). Philadelphia: University of Pennsylvania, August.

Houser, Trevor. 2010a. *Copenhagen, the Accord, and the Way Forward.* Policy Briefs in International Economics 10-5. Washington: Peterson Institute for International Economics.

Houser, Trevor. 2010b. Less Can Be More: Protecting Cancún's Fragile Victory. RealTime Economic Issues Watch (December 15). Washington: Peterson Institute for International Economics.

IEA (International Energy Agency). 2009a. *Energy Balances of OECD Countries* (2006 ed.) and *Energy Balances of Non-OECD Countries* (2006 ed.). Paris. Available at www.iea.org.

IEA (International Energy Agency). 2009b. *World Energy Outlook 2009.* Paris.

IMF (International Monetary Fund). 2010. *World Economic Outlook* (October). Washington.

IPCC (Intergovernmental Panel on Climate Change). 2001. *Climate Change 2001: The Physical Science Basis.* Cambridge, UK: Cambridge University Press.

IPCC (Intergovernmental Panel on Climate Change). 2007a. *Climate Change 2007: The Physical Science Basis.* Cambridge, UK: Cambridge University Press.

IPCC (Intergovernmental Panel on Climate Change). 2007b. *Climate Change 2007: Mitigation of Climate Change.* Cambridge, UK: Cambridge University Press.

Kump, Lee R., Alexander Pavlov, and Michael A. Arthur. 2005. Massive Release of Hydrogen Sulfide to the Surface Ocean and Atmosphere during Intervals of Oceanic Anoxia. *Geology* 33: 397–400.

McKibbin, Warwick J., Adele Morris, and Peter J. Wilcoxen. 2010. *Comparing Climate Commitments: A Model-Based Analysis of the Copenhagen Accord.* Harvard Project on International Climate Agreements, Discussion Paper 10-36 (June). Cambridge, MA: Harvard University.

McKinsey & Company. 2009. *Pathways to a Low-Carbon Economy: Version 2 of the Global Greenhouse Gas Abatement Cost Curve* (January). New York. Available at https://solutions.mckinsey.com.

Myhre, G., K. Alterskjaer, and D. Lowe. 2010. Addendum to "A Fast Method for Updating Global Fossil Fuel Carbon Dioxide Emissions." *Environmental Research Letters* 5, no. 3.

Nakićenović, N., et al. 2000. *IPCC Special Report on Emissions Scenarios.* Cambridge, UK: Cambridge University Press.

NOAA (National Oceanic and Atmospheric Administration). 2011. *Trends in Atmospheric Carbon Dioxide—Mauna Loa*. Washington: US Department of Commerce (December). Available at http://www.esrl.noaa.gov/gmd/ccgg/trends.

Nordhaus, William. 2008. *A Question of Balance: Weighing the Options on Global Warming Policies*. New Haven, CT: Yale University Press.

Nordhaus, William. 2010a. Economic Aspects of Global Warming in a Post-Copenhagen Environment. *Proceedings of the National Academy of Sciences, PNAS Early Edition* (May). Washington. Available at www.pnas.org.

Nordhaus, William. 2010b. RICE-2010 Model. New Haven: Yale University (May). Available at http://nordhaus.econ.yale.edu/RICEmodels.htm.

Sheehan, Peter. 2008. The New Global Growth Path: Implications for Climate Change Analysis and Policy. *Climatic Change* 91: 211–31.

Stavins, Robert N. 2010. Why Cancun Trumped Copenhagen: Warmer Relations on Rising Temperatures. *Christian Science Monitor* (December 20).

Stern, Nicholas. 2007. *The Economics of Climate Change: The Stern Review*. Cambridge, UK: Cambridge University Press.

Subramanian, Arvind. 2010. *New PPP-Based Estimates of Renminbi Undervaluation and Policy Implications*. Policy Briefs in International Economics 10-8 (April). Washington: Peterson Institute for International Economics.

UNDP (United Nations Development Program). 2007. *Human Development Report 2007/2008: Fighting Climate Change—Human Solidarity in a Divided World*. New York: Palgrave Macmillan.

UNFCCC (United Nations Framework Convention on Climate Change). 2007. *Climate Change: Impacts, Vulnerabilities, and Adaptation in Developing Countries*. Bonn.

UNFCCC (United Nations Framework Convention on Climate Change). 2010a. *Copenhagen Accord*. Available at http://unfccc.int.

UNFCCC (United Nations Framework Convention on Climate Change). 2010b. *Outcome of the Work of the Ad Hoc Working Group on Long-Term Cooperative Action under the Convention*. Available at http://unfccc.int.

United Nations. 2010. *Report of the Secretary-General's High-Level Advisory Group on Climate Change Financing* (November). New York.

US Census Bureau. 2009. International Data Base. Washington. Available at www.census.gov/ipc/www/idb.

Van Vuuren, Detlef P., and Keywan Riahi. 2008. Do Recent Emissions Trends Imply Higher Emissions Forever? *Climatic Change* 91: 237–48.

Weitzman, Martin. 2007. A Review of the *Stern Review on the Economics of Climate Change*. *Journal of Economic Literature* 45, no. 3 (September): 703–24.

World Bank. 2010a. *World Development Report 2010: Development and Climate Change*. Washington.

World Bank. 2010b. *The Cost to Developing Countries of Adapting to Climate Change: New Methods and Estimates*. Washington.

World Resources Institute. 2009. *Energy Consumption: Total Energy Consumption*. Washington. Available at http://earthtrends.wri.org.

World Resources Institute. 2010. Climate Analysis Indicators Tool. Washington. Available at http://cait.wri.org.

Index

Ackerman et al. CRED model, 30, 31t
adaptation costs, 5
  financing, 79–80, 82–86
aerosols, 18, 103–105, 104t
agency problems, 26
agriculture, adaptation costs in, 79n
Algeria, emissions levels, 86
alternative policy scenarios, 34, 50–55, 53f. See
  also specific scenario
  abatement costs, 113t–116t
  atmospheric carbon dioxide concentrations,
    99–101, 100f
  discounted present value, 68–70, 69t
  emissions paths, 107, 108t–111t
atmospheric carbon dioxide concentrations,
  55, 55t, 99–101, 100f
Australia
  emissions paths, 35, 37t
  policy pledge, 20, 21t

Bangladesh, emissions levels, 86
Ban Ki-moon, 83
baseline per capita GDP, 94t–95t
Bolivia, 24
bottom-up cost models, 25–26
Brazil
  emissions trading, 58, 62
  marginal costs, 59
  policy pledge, 20–22, 21t
Brown, Gordon, 82
building sector, 72–73

business as usual (bau) baseline energy
  consumption, 97t–87t
business as usual (bau) emissions baseline, 2,
  7–18
  atmospheric concentration, 55, 55t, 99–101,
    100f
  Copenhagen Accord and, 22–23
  Copenhagen Convergence scenario, 33, 35,
    36f, 37t
  cost models, 39, 40t
  cumulative emissions, 55, 55t
  emissions trading, 66, 67t
  framework, 7–9
  growth decomposition
    1990–2006, 9, 10t–11t
    through 2030, 12–16, 13t–15t
    through 2050, 16–18, 17t
  other greenhouse gases and aerosols,
    103–105, 104t
  per capita, 96t

Canada
  emissions paths, 35, 37t
  policy pledge, 20, 21t
Cancún Adaptation Framework, 24
Cancún Agreements, 1–2, 23–24, 82
carbon abatement
  costs (See cost models)
  efficiency of (See efficiency)
  financing issues (See financing; investment
    requirements)

initiatives (*See* Cancún Agreements; Copenhagen Accord)
policy scenarios, 1–2
    alternative (*See* alternative policy scenarios)
    Copenhagen Convergence (*See* Copenhagen Convergence scenario)
    political issues and, 4, 80
carbon abatement study
  data sources and statistical tables, 91, 92t–98t
  estimates of, 83–87
  method and plan of, 2–3
  principal findings, 3–5
  synthesis, 81–87
carbon dioxide emissions
  atmospheric concentrations, 55, 55t, 99–101, 100f
  baseline (*See* business as usual emissions baseline)
  of Copenhagen Accord adherents, 86–87
  of Copenhagen Accord nonadherents, 86
  cumulative, 55, 55t
  individual versus country-level, 51
  population growth rates and, 15t, 16, 92t–93t
  sources of, 18
  time path of
      Copenhagen Convergence scenario, 33, 35, 36f, 37t
      framework, 8–9
  trading (*See* trade)
carbon dioxide price. *See* shadow price of carbon dioxide
"carbon fertilization" benefits, 1
"carbon leakage," 20
"carbon offset" payments, 3, 59, 63n, 85, 85t
Chakravarty scenario, 34, 51, 53f
  abatement costs, 115t
  atmospheric concentration, 55, 55t
  cumulative emissions, 55, 55t
  emissions path, 107, 110t
China
  cost models, 41t, 43
  emissions growth rate, 9, 12
  emissions paths, 35, 36f, 37t
  emissions trading, 58, 62
  investment costs, 75–76, 79, 84–86
  marginal costs, 59
  policy pledge, 21t, 22–23
  UNDP scenario, 52, 54t
Clinton, Hillary, 82, 83n
coal-based power, 72–73
Congressional Budget Office, 58, 59, 62

Copenhagen Accord, 1
  nonadherents, 86–87
  policy pledges, 2, 20–23, 21t
    cost models, 39–48
    emissions paths, 35, 36f, 37t
  study findings on, 3–5, 81–83
  target warming ceiling, 34
Copenhagen Convergence (CopCon) scenario, 2–3, 34–39
  abatement costs, 39–50
      EMF 22 models, 43, 44t–45t, 48
      McKinsey model, 46–48, 47t
      other model–based estimates, 48–50
      RICE model, 39–43, 41t–42t, 48
  alternative paths (*See* alternative policy scenarios)
  atmospheric concentration, 55, 55t
  carbon dioxide price, 59, 60t–61t
  cumulative emissions, 55, 55t
  efficiency, 33, 35–36, 38t, 39
  emissions paths, 33, 35, 36f, 37t, 108t
  emissions trading, 57–59, 60t–61t
      with reallocation (*See* period reallocation)
  investment costs, 71, 76, 77t–78t, 129t–130t
  study estimates based on, 83, 84t
  versus UNDP scenario, 52, 54t, 55
cost-benefit analysis, 58
cost-minimizing reallocation. *See* period reallocation
cost models, 2, 4–5, 25–31
  adaptation costs, 5
  bau (*See* business as usual (bau) emissions baseline)
  bottom-up, 25–26 (*See also* McKinsey model)
  Copenhagen Convergence scenario, 39–48
  emissions trading, 3, 62–63, 64t–65t, 70
  emissions trading and (*See* trade)
  financing (*See* financing; investment requirements)
  marginal costs, 58–59, 60t–61t, 68
  through 2050, 33–55
  top-down, 25–26 (*See also* EMF 22 models; RICE model)
CSIRO scenario, 79
cumulative carbon dioxide emissions, 55, 55t

data sources, 91, 92t–98t
deforestation, 18, 18n
developed countries. *See also specific country*
  Copenhagen Accord pledge, 20, 21t
  Copenhagen Convergence scenario abatement costs, 39–48

alternative paths, 51–52, 53f
emissions trading, 58, 63, 70
developing countries. *See also specific country*
Copenhagen Accord nonadherents, 86–87
Copenhagen Accord pledges, 20–22, 21t
Copenhagen Convergence scenario
alternative paths, 51–52, 53f
cost models, 39–48
emissions paths, 35, 37t
EMF 22 models, 123
emissions trading, 58, 63, 66, 70
financing needs, 84, 85t
investment costs, 71, 74, 79, 84, 85t
marginal costs, 59
"dry" climate model (CSIRO), 79

economic cost, versus investment cost, 73
economic growth, 18
Economics of Adaptation to Climate Change
(EACC), 79
"economy-wide emissions targets," 20
efficiency, 3–4
Copenhagen Convergence scenario, 33,
35–36, 38t, 39
front-end loading for, 68
Egypt
emissions levels, 86
emissions trading, 66
emerging-market countries. *See* developing
countries
EMF 22 models, 27–28
Copenhagen Convergence scenario, 43,
44t–45t, 48
cost parameters, 27, 28t
data and statistical tables, 121–23,
124t–125t, 126f, 127t–129t
emissions trading, 66n, 70
investment costs, 71, 73, 76–79, 123,
129t–130t
marginal costs, 59, 68
versus RICE model, 28, 29f, 122
study estimates based on, 83, 84t
through 2050, 34
energy consumption, business as usual
baseline, 97t–87t
Energy Information Administration (EIA), 2,
4, 7, 12, 107
Energy Modeling Forum cost model. *see* EMF
22 models
energy-sector investment, 72–73
equations
bau emissions baseline, 8
EMF 22 models, 123
investment requirements, 75

McKinsey model, 30
RICE model, 26, 58–59
equity-based principle of equalization in per
capita emissions, 33
European Union
emissions paths, 35, 36f, 37t
emissions trading, 62
global costs estimate, 82
marginal costs, 59
policy pledge, 20, 21t
UNDP scenario, 52, 54t
exchange rates, 43

financing, 3, 5. *See also* investment
requirements
adaptation costs, 79–80, 82–86
developing countries needs, 84, 85t
fossil fuels, emissions from. *See* carbon dioxide
emissions
Frankel scenario, 34, 51–55, 53f
abatement costs, 116t
atmospheric concentration, 55, 55t
cumulative emissions, 55, 55t
emissions path, 107, 111t
front-end loading, 68

G-Cubed general equilibrium model, 49–50
GDP
baseline per capita, 94t–95t
cost models as percentage of, 55, 68, 69t
global financial crisis, 18
global warming, damages from, 1–2
Gradual Equalization Factor, 52
greenhouse gases, 18, 103–105, 104t

India
emissions trading, 62, 66
marginal costs, 59
policy pledge, 21t, 22–23
UNDP scenario, 52, 54t
individual emissions, versus country-level
emissions, 51
industrial countries. *See* developed countries
industrial processes, emissions from. *See*
carbon dioxide emissions
industrial sector, 72–73
infrastructure costs, 80
Integrated Assessment Models, 121
Intergovernmental Panel on Climate Change
(IPCC), 2
cost estimates, 48–49
SRES scenario, 99–101, 100f
targets, 34
Third Assessment Report, 99, 103

International Development Association, 80
International Energy Agency, 71–74
investment requirements, 3, 5, 71–79. *See also*
    financing
    components of, 82–83
    Copenhagen Convergence scenario, 71, 76,
        77t–78t, 129t–130t
    implied by cost estimates, 75–79
    sectoral composition of, 72–73
Iran
    emissions levels, 86
    policy scenario, 35, 37t
Iraq, emissions levels, 86

Japan
    emissions growth rate, 9
    emissions paths, 35, 37t
    emissions trading, 62
    policy pledge, 20, 21t

Kazakhstan, emissions paths, 35, 37t
Kuwait, emissions levels, 86
Kyoto Protocol, 1, 19, 24

land use, 18, 18n
Latecomer Catch-Up Factor, 52

Malaysia
    emissions paths, 35, 37t
    emissions levels, 86
marginal costs, 58–59, 60t–61t, 68
market imperfections, 26
McKinsey model, 30
    Copenhagen Convergence scenario, 46–48,
        47t
    cost parameters, 30, 31t
    investment costs, 74–75
MESSAGE model, 74–75
Mexico
    emissions trading, 58, 62
    marginal costs, 59
    policy pledge, 20–21, 21t

"nationally appropriate mitigation actions,"
    20
NCAR scenario, 79–80
Nigeria, emissions levels, 86
Nordhaus, William
    cost models (*See also* RICE model)
        Copenhagen Convergence, 48–49
    social rate of time preference, 66
North Korea, emissions levels, 86

offset payments, 3, 63n, 85, 85t

OGGA (other greenhouse gases and aerosols),
    18, 103–105, 104t

Pakistan
    emissions levels, 86
    emissions trading, 66
per capita emissions, equity-based principle of
    equalization in, 33
period reallocation
    abatement costs, 68, 69t, 83–84
    data and statistical tables, 117, 118t–120t
    emissions paths, 66–70, 67t
Philippines, emissions levels, 86
policy pledges, 2, 20–23, 21t, 35
    cost models, 39–48
    emissions paths, 35, 36f, 37t
policy scenarios, 1–2
    alternative (*See* alternative policy scenarios)
    Copenhagen Convergence (*See* Copenhagen
        Convergence scenario)
political issues, 4, 80
population growth rates, 15t, 16, 92t–93t
power sector, 72–73
Progressive Reduction Factor, 52

reallocation. *See* period reallocation
REMIND model, 74–75
RICE model, 4, 26–27
    Copenhagen Convergence scenario, 39–43,
        41t–42t, 48
        discounted present value, 68–70, 69t
    cost parameters, 26–27, 27t
    versus EMF 22 models, 28, 29f, 122
    emissions trading, 57, 62–63, 64t–65t
    investment costs, 71, 73, 76–79
    marginal costs, 58–59, 60t–61t, 68
    study estimates based on, 83, 84t
    through 2050, 33–34
Russia, emissions paths, 35, 37t

Saudi Arabia
    emissions levels, 86
    emissions paths, 35, 37t
shadow price of carbon dioxide, 5, 58–70
    under Copenhagen Convergence scenario,
        59, 60t–61t
    offset purchases, 85, 85t
    time path of, 66–68, 67t
social benefits, 58n
social rate of time preference, 66, 66n
South Africa
    emissions paths, 35, 37t
    policy pledge, 20–21, 21t
South Korea

emissions paths, 35, 37*t*
emissions trading, 58, 62
policy pledge, 20–21, 21*t*
Special Report on Emissions Scenarios (SRES) scenario, 99–101, 100*f*
Stanford Energy Modeling Forum (EMF) cost model. *see* EMF 22 models

Taiwan, emissions levels, 86
target warming ceiling, 34
Thailand
   emissions levels, 86
   emissions paths, 35, 37*t*
time path
   carbon dioxide price, 66–68, 67*t*
   cost-minimizing reallocation (*See* period reallocation)
   emissions
      Copenhagen Convergence scenario, 33, 35, 36*f*, 37*t*
      framework, 8–9
top-down cost model, 25–26
trade, 57–70. *See also* shadow price of carbon dioxide
   Copenhagen Convergence scenario, 59, 60*t*–61*t*
   with reallocation (*See* period reallocation)
   RICE model, 57, 62–63, 64*t*–65*t*
transport sector, 72–73
Turkey, emissions levels, 86

Ukraine, emissions paths, 35, 37*t*
United Nations Development Program (UNDP) scenario, 34, 50–51, 53*f*
   abatement costs, 113*t*–114*t*

atmospheric concentration, 55, 55*t*
versus Copenhagen Convergence, 52, 54*t*, 55
cumulative emissions, 55, 55*t*
emissions path, 107, 109*t*
United Nations Framework Convention on Climate Change (UNFCCC). *See* Cancún Agreements; Copenhagen Accord
United States
   Copenhagen Accord pledge, 20, 21*t*
   emissions paths, 35, 36*f*, 37*t*
   emissions trading, 62
   global costs estimate, 82
   marginal costs, 59
   UNDP scenario, 52, 54*t*
   Waxman-Markey bill (*See* Waxman-Markey bill)
US Census Bureau, 16
Uzbekistan, emissions levels, 86

Venezuela, emissions levels, 86
Vietnam, emissions levels, 86

Waxman-Markey bill (US)
   climate legislation since, 24
   emissions trading, 5, 58, 59, 62, 63*n*
   targets, 20
"wet" climate model (NCAR), 79–80
World Bank
   adaptation costs, 79, 84–85
   investment requirements, 71, 74–75
   market exchange rates, 43
   World Development Report (WDR), 74

Other Publications from the Peterson Institute for International Economics

WORKING PAPERS

94-1 APEC and Regional Trading Arrangements in the Pacific Jeffrey A. Frankel with Shang-Jin Wei and Ernesto Stein

94-2 Towards an Asia Pacific Investment Code Edward M. Graham

94-3 Merchandise Trade in the APEC Region: Is There Scope for Liberalization on an MFN Basis? Paul Wonnacott

94-4 The Automotive Industry in Southeast Asia: Can Protection Be Made Less Costly? Paul Wonnacott

94-5 Implications of Asian Economic Growth Marcus Noland

95-1 APEC: The Bogor Declaration and the Path Ahead C. Fred Bergsten

95-2 From Bogor to Miami...and Beyond: Regionalism in the Asia Pacific and the Western Hemisphere Jeffrey J. Schott

95-3 Has Asian Export Performance Been Unique? Marcus Noland

95-4 Association of Southeast Asian Nations and ASEAN Free Trade Area: Chronology and Statistics Gautam Jaggi

95-5 The North Korean Economy Marcus Noland

95-6 China and the International Economic System Marcus Noland

96-1 APEC after Osaka: Toward Free Trade by 2010/2020 C. Fred Bergsten

96-2 Public Policy, Private Preferences, and the Japanese Trade Pattern Marcus Noland

96-3 German Lessons for Korea: The Economics of Unification Marcus Noland

96-4 Research and Development Activities and Trade Specialization in Japan Marcus Noland

96-5 China's Economic Reforms: Chronology and Statistics Gautam Jaggi, Mary Rundle, Daniel H. Rosen, and Yuichi Takahashi

96-6 US-China Economic Relations Marcus Noland

96-7 The Market Structure Benefits of Trade and Investment Liberalization Raymond Atje and Gary Clyde Hufbauer

96-8 The Future of US-Korea Economic Relations Marcus Noland

96-9 Competition Policies in the Dynamic Industrializing Economies: The Case of China, Korea, and Chinese Taipei Edward M. Graham

96-10 Modeling Economic Reform in North Korea Marcus Noland, Sherman Robinson, and Monica Scatasta

96-11 Trade, Investment, and Economic Conflict Between the United States and Asia Marcus Noland

96-12 APEC in 1996 and Beyond: The Subic Summit C. Fred Bergsten

96-13 Some Unpleasant Arithmetic Concerning Unification Marcus Noland

96-14 Restructuring Korea's Financial Sector for Greater Competitiveness Marcus Noland

96-15 Competitive Liberalization and Global Free Trade: A Vision for the 21st Century C. Fred Bergsten

97-1 Chasing Phantoms: The Political Economy of USTR Marcus Noland

97-2 US-Japan Civil Aviation: Prospects for Progress Jacqueline McFadyen

97-3 Open Regionalism C. Fred Bergsten

97-4 Lessons from the Bundesbank on the Occasion of Its 40th (and Second to Last?) Birthday Adam S. Posen

97-5 The Economics of Korean Unification Marcus Noland, Sherman Robinson, and Li-Gang Liu

98-1 The Costs and Benefits of Korean Unification Marcus Noland, Sherman Robinson, and Li-Gang Liu

98-2 Asian Competitive Devaluations Li-Gang Liu, Marcus Noland, Sherman Robinson, and Zhi Wang

98-3 Fifty Years of the GATT/WTO: Lessons from the Past for Strategies or the Future C. Fred Bergsten

98-4 NAFTA Supplemental Agreements: Four Year Review Jacqueline McFadyen

98-5 Local Government Spending: Solving the Mystery of Japanese Fiscal Packages Hiroko Ishii and Erika Wada

98-6 The Global Economic Effects of the Japanese Crisis Marcus Noland, Sherman Robinson, and Zhi Wang

98-7 The Relationship Between Trade and Foreign Investment: Empirical Results for Taiwan and South Korea Li-Gang Liu, The World Bank, and Edward M. Graham

99-1 Rigorous Speculation: The Collapse and Revival of the North Korean Economy Marcus Noland, Sherman Robinson, and Tao Wang

99-2 Famine in North Korea: Causes and Cures   Marcus Noland, Sherman Robinson, and Tao Wang

99-3 Competition Policy and FDI: A Solution in Search of a Problem?   Marcus Noland

99-4 The Continuing Asian Financial Crisis: Global Adjustment and Trade   Marcus Noland, Sherman Robinson, and Zhi Wang

99-5 Why EMU Is Irrelevant for the German Economy   Adam S. Posen

99-6 The Global Trading System and the Developing Countries in 2000   C. Fred Bergsten

99-7 Modeling Korean Unification   Marcus Noland, Sherman Robinson, and Tao Wang

99-8 Sovereign Liquidity Crisis: The Strategic Case for a Payments Standstill   Marcus Miller and Lei Zhang

99-9 The Case for Joint Management of Exchange Rate Flexibility   C. Fred Bergsten, Olivier Davanne, and Pierre Jacquet

99-10 Does Talk Matter After All? Inflation Targeting and Central Bank Behavior   Kenneth N. Kuttner and Adam S. Posen

99-11 Hazards and Precautions: Tales of International Finance   Gary Clyde Hufbauer and Erika Wada

99-12 The Globalization of Services: What Has Happened? What Are the Implications?   Gary Clyde Hufbauer and Tony Warren

00-1 Regulatory Standards in the WTO   Keith Maskus

00-2 International Economic Agreements and the Constitution   Richard M. Goodman and John M. Frost

00-3 Electronic Commerce in Developing Countries   Catherine L. Mann

00-4 The New Asian Challenge   C. Fred Bergsten

00-5 How the Sick Man Avoided Pneumonia: The Philippines in the Asian Financial Crisis   Marcus Noland

00-6 Inflation, Monetary Transparency, and G-3 Exchange Rate Volatility   Kenneth N. Kuttner and Adam S. Posen

00-7 Transatlantic Issues in Electronic Commerce   Catherine L. Mann

00-8 Strengthening the International Financial Architecture: Where Do We Stand?   Morris Goldstein

00-9 On Currency Crises and Contagion   Marcel Fratzscher

01-1 Price Level Convergence and Inflation in Europe   John H. Rogers, Gary Clyde Hufbauer, and Erika Wada

01-2 Subsidies, Market Closure, Cross-Border Investment, and Effects on Competition: The Case of FDI on the Telecommunications Sector   Edward M. Graham

01-3 Foreign Direct Investment in China: Effects on Growth and Economic Performance   Edward M. Graham and Erika Wada

01-4 IMF Structural Conditionality: How Much Is Too Much?   Morris Goldstein

01-5 Unchanging Innovation and Changing Economic Performance in Japan   Adam S. Posen

01-6 Rating Banks in Emerging Markets   Liliana Rojas-Suarez

01-7 Beyond Bipolar: A Three-Dimensional Assessment of Monetary Frameworks   Kenneth N. Kuttner and Adam S. Posen

01-8 Finance and Changing US-Japan Relations: Convergence Without Leverage—Until Now   Adam S. Posen

01-9 Macroeconomic Implications of the New Economy   Martin Neil Baily

01-10 Can International Capital Standards Strengthen Banks in Emerging Markets?   Liliana Rojas-Suarez

02-1 Moral Hazard and the US Stock Market: Analyzing the "Greenspan Put"?   Marcus Miller, Paul Weller, and Lei Zhang

02-2 Passive Savers and Fiscal Policy Effectiveness in Japan   Kenneth N. Kuttner and Adam S. Posen

02-3 Home Bias, Transaction Costs, and Prospects for the Euro: A More Detailed Analysis   Catherine L. Mann and Ellen E. Meade

02-4 Toward a Sustainable FTAA: Does Latin America Meet the Necessary Financial Preconditions?   Liliana Rojas-Suarez

02-5 Assessing Globalization's Critics: "Talkers Are No Good Doers???"   Kimberly Ann Elliott, Debayani Kar, and J. David Richardson

02-6 Economic Issues Raised by Treatment of Takings under NAFTA Chapter 11   Edward M. Graham

03-1 Debt Sustainability, Brazil, and the IMF   Morris Goldstein

03-2 Is Germany Turning Japanese?   Adam S. Posen

03-3 Survival of the Best Fit: Exposure to Low-Wage Countries and the (Uneven) Growth of US Manufacturing Plants   Andrew B. Bernard, J. Bradford Jensen, and Peter K. Schott

03-4 Falling Trade Costs, Heterogeneous Firms, and Industry Dynamics   Andrew B. Bernard, J. Bradford Jensen, and Peter K. Schott

03-5 Famine and Reform in North Korea   Marcus Noland

03-6 Empirical Investigations in Inflation Targeting   Yifan Hu

03-7 Labor Standards and the Free Trade Area of the Americas   Kimberly Ann Elliott

03-8 Religion, Culture, and Economic
Performance   Marcus Noland
03-9 It Takes More than a Bubble to Become
Japan   Adam S. Posen
03-10 The Difficulty of Discerning What's
Too Tight: Taylor Rules and Japanese
Monetary Policy   `Adam S. Posen and
Kenneth N. Kuttner
04-1 Adjusting China's Exchange Rate
Policies   Morris Goldstein
04-2 Popular Attitudes, Globalization, and
Risk   Marcus Noland
04-3 Selective Intervention and Growth: The
Case of Korea   Marcus Noland
05-1 Outsourcing and Offshoring: Pushing
the European Model Over the Hill,
Rather Than Off the Cliff!
Jacob Funk Kirkegaard
05-2 China's Role in the Revived Bretton
Woods System: A Case of Mistaken
Identity   Morris Goldstein and
Nicholas R. Lardy
05-3 Affinity and International Trade
Marcus Noland
05-4 South Korea's Experience with
International Capital Flows
Marcus Noland
05-5 Explaining Middle Eastern
Authoritarianism   Marcus Noland
05-6 Postponing Global Adjustment: An
Analysis of the Pending Adjustment of
Global Imbalances   Edwin M. Truman
05-7 What Might the Next Emerging Market
Financial Crisis Look Like?
Morris Goldstein, assisted by Anna Wong
05-8 Egypt after the Multi-Fiber
Arrangement: Global Approval and
Textile Supply Chains as a Route for
Industrial Upgrading   Dan Magder
05-9 Tradable Services: Understanding
the Scope and Impact of Services
Offshoring   J. Bradford Jensen and
Lori G. Kletzer
05-10 Importers, Exporters, and
Multinationals: A Portrait of Firms in
the US that Trade Goods
Andrew B. Bernard, J. Bradford Jensen,
and Peter K. Schott
05-11 The US Trade Deficit: A Disaggregated
Perspective   Catherine L. Mann and
Katharina Plück
05-12 Prospects for Regional Free Trade in
Asia   Gary Clyde Hufbauer and
Yee Wong
05-13 Predicting Trade Expansion under FTAs
and Multilateral Agreements
Dean A. DeRosa and John P. Gilbert
05-14 The East Asian Industrial Policy
Experience: Implications for the Middle
East   Marcus Noland and Howard Pack
05-15 Outsourcing and Skill Imports: Foreign
High-Skilled Workers on H-1B and L-1
Visas in the United States
Jacob Funk Kirkegaard

06-1 Why Central Banks Should Not Burst
Bubbles   Adam S. Posen
06-2 The Case for an International Reserve
Diversification Standard
Edwin M. Truman and Anna Wong
06-3 Offshoring in Europe—Evidence of a
Two-Way Street from Denmark
Peter Ørberg Jensen, Jacob Funk
Kirkegaard, and Nicolai Søndergaard
Laugesen
06-4 The External Policy of the Euro Area:
Organizing for Foreign Exchange
Intervention   C. Randall Henning
06-5 The Eurasian Growth Paradox
Anders Åslund and Nazgul Jenish
06-6 Has EMU Had Any Impact on the
Degree of Wage Restraint?
Adam S. Posen and Daniel Popov Gould
06-7 Firm Structure, Multinationals, and
Manufacturing Plant Deaths
Andrew B. Bernard and J. Bradford Jensen
07-1 The Trade Effects of Preferential
Arrangements: New Evidence from the
Australia Productivity Commission
Dean A. DeRosa
07-2 Offshoring, Outsourcing, and
Production Relocation—Labor-Market
Effects in the OECD Countries and
Developing Asia Jacob Funk Kirkegaard
07-3 Do Markets Care Who Chairs the
Central Bank?   Kenneth N. Kuttner and
Adam S. Posen
07-4 Industrial Policy, Innovative Policy,
and Japanese Competitiveness: Japan's
Pursuit of Competitive Advantage
Marcus Noland
07-5 A (Lack of) Progress Report on China's
Exchange Rate Policies Morris Goldstein
07-6 Measurement and Inference in
International Reserve Diversification
Anna Wong
07-7 North Korea's External Economic
Relations   Stephan Haggard and
Marcus Noland
07-8 Congress, Treasury, and the
Accountability of Exchange Rate Policy:
How the 1988 Trade Act Should Be
Reformed   C. Randall Henning
07-9 Merry Sisterhood or Guarded
Watchfulness? Cooperation Between the
International Monetary Fund and the
World Bank   Michael Fabricius
08-1 Exit Polls: Refugee Assessments of
North Korea's Transitions
Yoonok Chang, Stephan Haggard, and
Marcus Noland
08-2 Currency Undervaluation and Sovereign
Wealth Funds: A New Role for the WTO
Aaditya Mattoo and Arvind Subramanian
08-3 Exchange Rate Economics
John Williamson
08-4 Migration Experiences of North Korean
Refugees: Survey Evidence from China
Yoonok Chang, Stephan Haggard, and
Marcus Noland

08-5 Korean Institutional Reform in Comparative Perspective
Marcus Noland and Erik Weeks

08-6 Estimating Consistent Fundamental Equilibrium Exchange Rates
William R. Cline

08-7 Policy Liberalization and FDI Growth, 1982 to 2006   Matthew Adler and Gary Clyde Hufbauer

08-8 Multilateralism Beyond Doha
Aaditya Mattoo and Arvind Subramanian

08-9 Famine in North Korea Redux?
Stephan Haggard and Marcus Noland

08-10 Recent Trade Patterns and Modes of Supply in Computer and Information Services in the United States and NAFTA Partners   Jacob Funk Kirkegaard

08-11 On What Terms Is the IMF Worth Funding?   Edwin M. Truman

08-12 The (Non) Impact of UN Sanctions on North Korea   Marcus Noland

09-1 The GCC Monetary Union: Choice of Exchange Rate Regime   Mohsin S. Khan

09-2 Policy Liberalization and US Merchandise Trade Growth, 1980–2006
Gary Clyde Hufbauer and Matthew Adler

09-3 American Multinationals and American Economic Interests: New Dimensions to an Old Debate   Theodore H. Moran

09-4 Sanctioning North Korea: The Political Economy of Denuclearization and Proliferation   Stephan Haggard and Marcus Noland

09-5 Structural and Cyclical Trends in Net Employment over US Business Cycles, 1949–2009: Implications for the Next Recovery and Beyond
Jacob Funk Kirkegaard

09-6 What's on the Table? The Doha Round as of August 2009   Matthew Adler, Claire Brunel, Gary Clyde Hufbauer, and Jeffrey J. Schott

09-7 Criss-Crossing Globalization: Uphill Flows of Skill-Intensive Goods and Foreign Direct Investment
Aaditya Mattoo and Arvind Subramanian

09-8 Reform from Below: Behavioral and Institutional Change in North Korea
Stephan Haggard and Marcus Noland

09-9 The World Trade Organization and Climate Change: Challenges and Options   Gary Clyde Hufbauer and Jisun Kim

09-10 A Tractable Model of Precautionary Reserves, Net Foreign Assets, or Sovereign Wealth Funds
Christopher D. Carroll and Olivier Jeanne

09-11 The Impact of the Financial Crisis on Emerging Asia   Morris Goldstein and Daniel Xie

09-12 Capital Flows to Developing Countries: The Allocation Puzzle
Pierre-Olivier Gourinchas and Olivier Jeanne

09-13 Mortgage Loan Modifications: Program Incentives and Restructuring Design
Dan Magder

09-14 It Should Be a Breeze: Harnessing the Potential of Open Trade and Investment Flows in the Wind Energy Industry
Jacob Funk Kirkegaard, Thilo Hanemann, and Lutz Weischer

09-15 Reconciling Climate Change and Trade Policy   Aaditya Mattoo, Arvind Subramanian, Dominique van der Mensbrugghe, and Jianwu He

09-16 The International Monetary Fund and Regulatory Challenges
Edwin M. Truman

10-1 Estimation of De Facto Flexibility Parameter and Basket Weights in Evolving Exchange Rate Regimes
Jeffrey Frankel and Daniel Xie

10-2 Economic Crime and Punishment in North Korea   Stephan Haggard and Marcus Noland

10-3 Intra-Firm Trade and Product Contractibility   Andrew B. Bernard, J. Bradford Jensen, Stephen J. Redding, and Peter K. Schott

10-4 The Margins of US Trade
Andrew B. Bernard, J. Bradford Jensen, Stephen J. Redding, and Peter K. Schott

10-5 Excessive Volatility in Capital Flows: A Pigouvian Taxation Approach
Olivier Jeanne and Anton Korinek

10-6 Toward a Sunny Future? Global Integration in the Solar PV Industry
Jacob Funk Kirkegaard, Thilo Hanemann, Lutz Weischer, Matt Miller

10-7 The Realities and Relevance of Japan's Great Recession: Neither Ran nor Rashomon   Adam S. Posen

10-8 Do Developed and Developing Countries Compete Head to Head in High Tech?   Lawrence Edwards and Robert Z. Lawrence

10-9 US Trade and Wages: The Misleading Implications of Conventional Trade Theory   Lawrence Edwards and Robert Z. Lawrence

10-10 Wholesalers and Retailers in US Trade
Andrew B. Bernard, J. Bradford Jensen, Stephen J. Redding, and Peter K. Schott

10-11 The Design and Effects of Monetary Policy in Sub-Saharan African Countries
Mohsin S. Khan

10-12 Managing Credit Booms and Busts: A Pigouvian Taxation Approach
Olivier Jeanne and Anton Korinek

10-13 The G-20 and International Financial Institution Governance
Edwin M. Truman

10-14 Reform of the Global Financial Architecture   Garry J. Schinasi and Edwin M. Truman

10-15 A Role for the G-20 in Addressing Climate Change?   Trevor Houser

10-16 Exchange Rate Policy in Brazil
John Williamson

10-17 Trade Disputes Between China and the United States: Growing Pains so Far, Worse Ahead?
Gary Clyde Hufbauer and Jared C. Woollacott

10-18 Sovereign Bankruptcy in the European Union in the Comparative Perspective
Leszek Balcerowicz

11-1 Current Account Imbalances Coming Back
Joseph Gagnon

11-2 Too Big to Fail: The Transatlantic Debate
Morris Goldstein and Nicolas Véron

11-3 Foreign Direct Investment in Times of Crisis
Lauge Skovgaard Poulsen and Gary Clyde Hufbauer

11-4 A Generalized Fact and Model of Long-Run Economic Growth: Kaldor Fact as a Special Case
Daniel Danxia Xie

11-5 Integrating Reform of Financial Regulation with Reform of the International Monetary System
Morris Goldstein

11-6 Capital Account Liberalization and the Role of the RMB
Nicholas Lardy and Patrick Douglass

11-7 Capital Controls: Myth and Reality — A Portfolio Balance Approach
Nicolas E. Magud, Carmen M. Reinhart, and Kenneth S. Rogoff

11-8 Resource Management and Transition in Central Asia, Azerbaijan, and Mongolia
Richard Pomfret

11-9 Coordinating Regional and Multilateral Financial Institutions
C. Randall Henning

11-10 The Liquidation of Government Debt
Carmen M. Reinhart and M. Belen Sbrancia

11-11 Foreign Manufacturing Multinationals and the Transformation of the Chinese Economy: New Measurements, New Perspectives
Theodore H. Moran

POLICY BRIEFS

98-1 The Asian Financial Crisis
Morris Goldstein

98-2 The New Agenda with China
C. Fred Bergsten

98-3 Exchange Rates for the Dollar, Yen, and Euro
Simon Wren-Lewis

98-4 Sanctions-Happy USA
Gary Clyde Hufbauer

98-5 The Depressing News from Asia
Marcus Noland, Sherman Robinson, and Zhi Wang

98-6 The Transatlantic Economic Partnership
Ellen L. Frost

98-7 A New Strategy for the Global Crisis
C. Fred Bergsten

98-8 Reviving the "Asian Monetary Fund"
C. Fred Bergsten

99-1 Implementing Japanese Recovery
Adam S. Posen

99-2 A Radical but Workable Restructuring Plan for South Korea
Edward M. Graham

99-3 Crawling Bands or Monitoring Bands: How to Manage Exchange Rates in a World of Capital Mobility
John Williamson

99-4 Market Mechanisms to Reduce the Need for IMF Bailouts   Catherine L. Mann

99-5 Steel Quotas: A Rigged Lottery
Gary Clyde Hufbauer and Erika Wada

99-6 China and the World Trade Organization: An Economic Balance Sheet   Daniel H. Rosen

99-7 Trade and Income Distribution: The Debate and New Evidence
William R. Cline

99-8 Preserve the Exchange Stabilization Fund   C. Randall Henning

99-9 Nothing to Fear but Fear (of Inflation) Itself   Adam S. Posen

99-10 World Trade after Seattle: Implications for the United States
Gary Clyde Hufbauer

00-1 The Next Trade Policy Battle
C. Fred Bergsten

00-2 Decision-Making in the WTO
Jeffrey J. Schott and Jayashree Watal

00-3 American Access to China's Market: The Congressional Vote on PNTR
Gary Clyde Hufbauer and Daniel H. Rosen

00-4 Third Oil Shock: Real or Imaginary? Consequences and Policy Alternatives
Philip K. Verleger, Jr.

00-5 The Role of the IMF: A Guide to the Reports   John Williamson

00-6 The ILO and Enforcement of Core Labor Standards   Kimberly Ann Elliott

00-7 "No" to Foreign Telecoms Equals "No" to the New Economy!
Gary Clyde Hufbauer and Edward M. Graham

01-1 Brunei: A Turning Point for APEC?
C. Fred Bergsten

01-2 A Prescription to Relieve Worker Anxiety   Lori G. Kletzer and Robert E. Litan

01-3 The US Export-Import Bank: Time for an Overhaul   Gary Clyde Hufbauer

01-4 Japan 2001 — Decisive Action or Financial Panic   Adam S. Posen

01-5 Fin(d)ing Our Way on Trade and Labor Standards?   Kimberly Ann Elliott

01-6 Prospects for Transatlantic Competition Policy   Mario Monti

01-7 The International Implications of Paying Down the Debt   Edwin M. Truman

01-8 Dealing with Labor and Environment Issues in Trade Promotion Legislation
Kimberly Ann Elliott

01-9 Steel: Big Problems, Better Solutions
Gary Clyde Hufbauer and Ben Goodrich

01-10 Economic Policy Following the Terrorist Attacks Martin Neil Baily

01-11 Using Sanctions to Fight Terrorism
Gary Clyde Hufbauer, Jeffrey J. Schott, and Barbara Oegg

02-1 Time for a Grand Bargain in Steel?
Gary Clyde Hufbauer and Ben Goodrich

02-2 Prospects for the World Economy: From Global Recession to Global Recovery
Michael Mussa

02-3 Sovereign Debt Restructuring: New Articles, New Contracts — or No Change?
Marcus Miller

02-4 Support the Ex-Im Bank: It Has Work to Do! Gary Clyde Hufbauer and Ben Goodrich

02-5 The Looming Japanese Crisis
Adam S. Posen

02-6 Capital-Market Access: New Frontier in the Sanctions Debate
Gary Clyde Hufbauer and Barbara Oegg

02-7 Is Brazil Next? John Williamson

02-8 Further Financial Services Liberalization in the Doha Round? Wendy Dobson

02-9 Global Economic Prospects
Michael Mussa

02-10 The Foreign Sales Corporation: Reaching the Last Act?
Gary Clyde Hufbauer

03-1 Steel Policy: The Good, the Bad, and the Ugly Gary Clyde Hufbauer and Ben Goodrich

03-2 Global Economic Prospects: Through the Fog of Uncertainty Michael Mussa

03-3 Economic Leverage and the North Korean Nuclear Crisis
Kimberly Ann Elliott

03-4 The Impact of Economic Sanctions on US Trade: Andrew Rose's Gravity Model Gary Clyde Hufbauer and Barbara Oegg

03-5 Reforming OPIC for the 21st Century
Theodore H. Moran and C. Fred Bergsten

03-6 The Strategic Importance of US-Korea Economic Relations Marcus Noland

03-7 Rules Against Earnings Stripping: Wrong Answer to Corporate Inversions
Gary Clyde Hufbauer and Ariel Assa

03-8 More Pain, More Gain: Politics and Economics of Eliminating Tariffs
Gary Clyde Hufbauer and Ben Goodrich

03-9 EU Accession and the Euro: Close Together or Far Apart?
Peter B. Kenen and Ellen E. Meade

03-10 Next Move in Steel: Revocation or Retaliation? Gary Clyde Hufbauer and Ben Goodrich

03-11 Globalization of IT Services and White Collar Jobs: The Next Wave of Productivity Growth Catherine L. Mann

04-1 This Far and No Farther? Nudging Agricultural Reform Forward
Tim Josling and Dale Hathaway

04-2 Labor Standards, Development, and CAFTA Kimberly Ann Elliott

04-3 Senator Kerry on Corporate Tax Reform: Right Diagnosis, Wrong Prescription
Gary Clyde Hufbauer and Paul Grieco

04-4 Islam, Globalization, and Economic Performance in the Middle East
Marcus Noland and Howard Pack

04-5 China Bashing 2004
Gary Clyde Hufbauer and Yee Wong

04-6 What Went Right in Japan
Adam S. Posen

04-7 What Kind of Landing for the Chinese Economy? Morris Goldstein and Nicholas R. Lardy

05-1 A Currency Basket for East Asia, Not Just China John Williamson

05-2 After Argentina Anna Gelpern

05-3 Living with Global Imbalances: A Contrarian View Richard N. Cooper

05-4 The Case for a New Plaza Agreement
William R. Cline

06-1 The United States Needs German Economic Leadership Adam S. Posen

06-2 The Doha Round after Hong Kong
Gary Clyde Hufbauer and Jeffrey J. Schott

06-3 Russia's Challenges as Chair of the G-8
Anders Åslund

06-4 Negotiating the Korea–United States Free Trade Agreement Jeffrey J. Schott, Scott C. Bradford, and Thomas Moll

06-5 Can Doha Still Deliver on the Development Agenda?
Kimberly Ann Elliott

06-6 China: Toward a Consumption Driven Growth Path Nicholas R. Lardy

06-7 Completing the Doha Round
Jeffrey J. Schott

06-8 Choosing Monetary Arrangements for the 21st Century: Problems of a Small Economy John Williamson

06-9 Can America Still Compete or Does It Need a New Trade Paradigm?
Martin Neil Baily and Robert Z. Lawrence

07-1 The IMF Quota Formula: Linchpin of Fund Reform Richard N. Cooper and Edwin M. Truman

07-2 Toward a Free Trade Area of the Asia Pacific C. Fred Bergsten

07-3 China and Economic Integration in East Asia: Implications for the United States
C. Fred Bergsten

07-4 Global Imbalances: Time for Action
Alan Ahearne, William R. Cline, Kyung Tae Lee, Yung Chul Park, Jean Pisani-Ferry, and John Williamson

07-5 American Trade Politics in 2007: Building Bipartisan Compromise I. M. Destler

07-6 Sovereign Wealth Funds: The Need for Greater Transparency and Accountability Edwin M. Truman

07-7 The Korea-US Free Trade Agreement: A Summary Assessment Jeffrey J. Schott

07-8 The Case for Exchange Rate Flexibility in Oil-Exporting Economies Brad Setser

08-1 "Fear" and Offshoring: The Scope and Potential Impact of Imports and Exports of Services J. Bradford Jensen and Lori G. Kletzer

08-2 Strengthening Trade Adjustment Assistance Howard F. Rosen

08-3 A Blueprint for Sovereign Wealth Fund Best Practices Edwin M. Truman

08-4 A Security and Peace Mechanism for Northeast Asia: The Economic Dimension Stephan Haggard and Marcus Noland

08-5 World Trade at Risk C. Fred Bergsten

08-6 North Korea on the Precipice of Famine Stephan Haggard, Marcus Noland, and Erik Weeks

08-7 New Estimates of Fundamental Equilibrium Exchange Rates William R. Cline and John Williamson

08-8 Financial Repression in China Nicholas R. Lardy

09-1 Did Reagan Rule In Vain? A Closer Look at True Expenditure Levels in the United States and Europe Jacob Funk Kirkegaard

09-2 Buy American: Bad for Jobs, Worse for Reputation Gary Clyde Hufbauer and Jeffrey J. Schott

09-3 A Green Global Recovery? Assessing US Economic Stimulus and the Prospects for International Coordination Trevor Houser, Shashank Mohan, and Robert Heilmayr

09-4 Money for the Auto Industry: Consistent with WTO Rules? Claire Brunel and Gary Clyde Hufbauer

09-5 The Future of the Chiang Mai Initiative: An Asian Monetary Fund? C. Randall Henning

09-6 Pressing the "Reset Button" on US-Russia Relations Anders Åslund and Andrew Kuchins

09-7 US Taxation of Multinational Corporations: What Makes Sense, What Doesn't Gary Clyde Hufbauer and Jisun Kim

09-8 Energy Efficiency in Buildings: A Global Economic Perspective Trevor Houser

09-9 The Alien Tort Statute of 1789: Time for a Fresh Look Gary Clyde Hufbauer

09-10 2009 Estimates of Fundamental Equilibrium Exchange Rates William R. Cline and John Williamson

09-11 Understanding Special Drawing Rights (SDRs) John Williamson

09-12 US Interests and the International Monetary Fund C. Randall Henning

09-13 A Solution for Europe's Banking Problem Adam S. Posen and Nicolas Véron

09-14 China's Changing Outbound Foreign Direct Investment Profile: Drivers and Policy Implication Daniel H. Rosen and Thilo Hanemann

09-15 India-Pakistan Trade: A Roadmap for Enhancing Economic Relations Mohsin S. Khan

09-16 Pacific Asia and the Asia Pacific: The Choices for APEC C. Fred Bergsten

09-17 The Economics of Energy Efficiency in Buildings Trevor Houser

09-18 Setting the NAFTA Agenda on Climate Change Jeffrey J. Schott and Meera Fickling

09-19 The 2008 Oil Price "Bubble" Mohsin S. Khan

09-20 Why SDRs Could Rival the Dollar John Williamson

09-21 The Future of the Dollar Richard N. Cooper

09-22 The World Needs Further Monetary Ease, Not an Early Exit Joseph E. Gagnon

10-1 The Winter of Their Discontent: Pyongyang Attacks the Market Stephan Haggard and Marcus Noland

10-2 Notes on Equilibrium Exchange Rates: William R. Cline and John Williamson

10-3 Confronting Asset Bubbles, Too Big to Fail, and Beggar-thy-Neighbor Exchange Rate Policies Morris Goldstein

10-4 After the Flop in Copenhagen Gary Clyde Hufbauer and Jisun Kim

10-5 Copenhagen, the Accord, and the Way Forward Trevor Houser

10-6 The Substitution Account as a First Step Toward Reform of the International Monetary System Peter B. Kenen

10-7 The Sustainability of China's Recovery from the Global Recession Nicholas R. Lardy

10-8 New PPP-Based Estimates of Renminbi Undervaluation and Policy Implications Arvind Subramanian

10-9 Protection by Stealth: Using the Tax Law to Discriminate against Foreign Insurance Companies Gary Clyde Hufbauer

10-10 Higher Taxes on US-Based Multinationals Would Hurt US Workers and Exports Gary Clyde Hufbauer and Theodore H. Moran

10-11 A Trade Agenda for the G-20 Jeffrey J. Schott

10-12 Assessing the American Power Act: The Economic, Employment, Energy Security and Environmental Impact of Senator Kerry and Senator Lieberman's Discussion Draft Trevor Houser, Shashank Mohan, and Ian Hoffman

10-13 Hobbling Exports and Destroying Jobs Gary Clyde Hufbauer and Theodore H. Moran

10-14 In Defense of Europe's Grand Bargain Jacob Funk Kirkegaard

10-15 Estimates of Fundamental Equilibrium Exchange Rates, May 2010 William R. Cline and John Williamson

10-16 Deepening China-Taiwan Relations through the Economic Cooperation Framework Agreement Daniel H. Rosen and Zhi Wang

10-17 The Big U-Turn: Japan Threatens to Reverse Postal Reforms Gary Clyde Hufbauer and Julia Muir

10-18 Dealing with Volatile Capital Flows Olivier Jeanne

10-19 Revisiting the NAFTA Agenda on Climate Change Jeffrey J. Schott and Meera Fickling

10-20 Renminbi Undervaluation, China's Surplus, and the US Trade Deficit William R. Cline

10-21 The Road to a Climate Change Agreement Runs Through Montreal Richard J. Smith

10-22 Not All Financial Regulation Is Global Stéphane Rottier and Nicolas Véron

10-23 Prospects for Implementing the Korea-US Free Trade Agreement Jeffrey J. Schott

10-24 The Central Banker's Case for Doing More Adam S. Posen

10-25 Will It Be Brussels, Berlin, or Financial Markets that Check Moral Hazard in Europe's Bailout Union? Most Likely the Latter! Jacob Funk Kirkegaard

10-26 Currency Wars? William R. Cline and John Williamson

10-27 How Europe Can Muddle Through Its Crisis Jacob Funk Kirkegaard

10-28 KORUS FTA 2.0: Assessing the Changes Jeffrey J. Schott

10-29 Strengthening IMF Surveillance: A Comprehensive Proposal Edwin M. Truman

10-30 An Update on EU Financial Reforms Nicolas Véron

11-1 Getting Surplus Countries to Adjust John Williamson

11-2 Corporate Tax Reform for a New Century Gary Clyde Hufbauer and Woan Foong Wong

11-3 The Elephant in the "Green Room": China and the Doha Round Aaditya Mattoo, Francis Ng, and Arvind Subramanian

11-4 The Outlook for International Monetary System Reform in 2011: A Preliminary Report Card Edwin M. Truman

11-5 Estimates of Fundamental Equilibrium Exchange Rates, May 2011 William R. Cline and John Williamson

11-6 Revitalizing the Export-Import Bank Gary Clyde Hufbauer, Meera Fickling, and Woan Foong Wong

* = out of print

POLICY ANALYSES IN INTERNATIONAL ECONOMICS Series

1 The Lending Policies of the International Monetary Fund* John Williamson August 1982 ISBN 0-88132-000-5

2 "Reciprocity": A New Approach to World Trade Policy?* William R. Cline September 1982 ISBN 0-88132-001-3

3 Trade Policy in the 1980s* C. Fred Bergsten and William R. Cline November 1982 ISBN 0-88132-002-1

4 International Debt and the Stability of the World Economy* William R. Cline September 1983 ISBN 0-88132-010-2

5 The Exchange Rate System,* 2d ed. John Williamson Sept. 1983, rev. June 1985 ISBN 0-88132-034-X

6 Economic Sanctions in Support of Foreign Policy Goals* Gary Clyde Hufbauer and Jeffrey J. Schott October 1983 ISBN 0-88132-014-5

7 A New SDR Allocation?* John Williamson March 1984 ISBN 0-88132-028-5

8 An International Standard for Monetary Stabilization* Ronald L. McKinnon March 1984 ISBN 0-88132-018-8

9 The Yen/Dollar Agreement: Liberalizing Japanese Capital Markets* Jeffrey Frankel December 1984 ISBN 0-88132-035-8

10 Bank Lending to Developing Countries: The Policy Alternatives* C. Fred Bergsten, William R. Cline, and John Williamson April 1985 ISBN 0-88132-032-3

11 Trading for Growth: The Next Round of Trade Negotiations* Gary Clyde Hufbauer and Jeffrey J. Schott September 1985 ISBN 0-88132-033-1

12 Financial Intermediation Beyond the Debt Crisis* Donald R. Lessard and John Williamson September 1985 ISBN 0-88132-021-8

13 The United States-Japan Economic Problem*   C. Fred Bergsten and William R. Cline
Oct. 1985, 2d ed. January 1987
ISBN 0-88132-060-9

14 Deficits and the Dollar: The World Economy at Risk*   Stephen Marris
Dec. 1985, 2d ed. November 1987
ISBN 0-88132-067-6

15 Trade Policy for Troubled Industries*
Gary Clyde Hufbauer and Howard F. Rosen
March 1986   ISBN 0-88132-020-X

16 The United States and Canada: The Quest for Free Trade*   Paul Wonnacott, with an appendix by John Williamson
March 1987   ISBN 0-88132-056-0

17 Adjusting to Success: Balance of Payments Policy in the East Asian NICs*
Bela Balassa and John Williamson
June 1987, rev. April 1990
ISBN 0-88132-101-X

18 Mobilizing Bank Lending to Debtor Countries*   William R. Cline
June 1987   ISBN 0-88132-062-5

19 Auction Quotas and United States Trade Policy*   C. Fred Bergsten, Kimberly Ann Elliott, Jeffrey J. Schott, and Wendy E. Takacs
September 1987   ISBN 0-88132-050-1

20 Agriculture and the GATT: Rewriting the Rules*   Dale E. Hathaway
September 1987   ISBN 0-88132-052-8

21 Anti-Protection: Changing Forces in United States Trade Politics*
I. M. Destler and John S. Odell
September 1987   ISBN 0-88132-043-9

22 Targets and Indicators: A Blueprint for the International Coordination of Economic Policy   John Williamson and Marcus H. Miller
September 1987   ISBN 0-88132-051-X

23 Capital Flight: The Problem and Policy Responses*   Donald R. Lessard and John Williamson
December 1987   ISBN 0-88132-059-5

24 United States-Canada Free Trade: An Evaluation of the Agreement*
Jeffrey J. Schott
April 1988   ISBN 0-88132-072-2

25 Voluntary Approaches to Debt Relief*
John Williamson
Sept. 1988, rev. May 1   ISBN 0-88132-098-6

26 American Trade Adjustment: The Global Impact*   William R. Cline
March 1989   ISBN 0-88132-095-1

27 More Free Trade Areas?*   Jeffrey J. Schott
May 1989   ISBN 0-88132-085-4

28 The Progress of Policy Reform in Latin America*   John Williamson
January 1990   ISBN 0-88132-100-1

29 The Global Trade Negotiations: What Can Be Achieved?*   Jeffrey J. Schott
September 1990   ISBN 0-88132-137-0

30 Economic Policy Coordination: Requiem for Prologue?*   Wendy Dobson
April 1991   ISBN 0-88132-102-8

31 The Economic Opening of Eastern Europe*
John Williamson
May 1991   ISBN 0-88132-186-9

32 Eastern Europe and the Soviet Union in the World Economy*   Susan Collins and Dani Rodrik
May 1991   ISBN 0-88132-157-5

33 African Economic Reform: The External Dimension*   Carol Lancaster
June 1991   ISBN 0-88132-096-X

34 Has the Adjustment Process Worked?*
Paul R. Krugman
October 1991   ISBN 0-88132-116-8

35 From Soviet DisUnion to Eastern Economic Community?*   Oleh Havrylyshyn and John Williamson
October 1991   ISBN 0-88132-192-3

36 Global Warming: The Economic Stakes*
William R. Cline
May 1992   ISBN 0-88132-172-9

37 Trade and Payments after Soviet Disintegration*   John Williamson
June 1992   ISBN 0-88132-173-7

38 Trade and Migration: NAFTA and Agriculture*   Philip L. Martin
October 1993   ISBN 0-88132-201-6

39 The Exchange Rate System and the IMF: A Modest Agenda   Morris Goldstein
June 1995   ISBN 0-88132-219-9

40 What Role for Currency Boards?
John Williamson
September 1995   ISBN 0-88132-222-9

41 Predicting External Imbalances for the United States and Japan*   William R. Cline
September 1995   ISBN 0-88132-220-2

42 Standards and APEC: An Action Agenda*
John S. Wilson
October 1995   ISBN 0-88132-223-7

43 Fundamental Tax Reform and Border Tax Adjustments*   Gary Clyde Hufbauer
January 1996   ISBN 0-88132-225-3

44 Global Telecom Talks: A Trillion Dollar Deal*   Ben A. Petrazzini
June 1996   ISBN 0-88132-230-X

45 WTO 2000: Setting the Course for World Trade   Jeffrey J. Schott
September 1996   ISBN 0-88132-234-2

46 The National Economic Council: A Work in Progress*   I. M. Destler
November 1996   ISBN 0-88132-239-3

47 The Case for an International Banking Standard   Morris Goldstein
April 1997   ISBN 0-88132-244-X

48 Transatlantic Trade: A Strategic Agenda*
Ellen L. Frost
May 1997   ISBN 0-88132-228-8

49 Cooperating with Europe's Monetary Union   C. Randall Henning
May 1997   ISBN 0-88132-245-8

50 Renewing Fast Track Legislation*
I. M. Destler
September 1997   ISBN 0-88132-252-0

51 Competition Policies for the Global
Economy   Edward M. Graham and
J. David Richardson
November 1997   ISBN 0-88132-249-0

52 Improving Trade Policy Reviews in the
World Trade Organization
Donald Keesing
April 1998   ISBN 0-88132-251-2

53 Agricultural Trade Policy: Completing the
Reform   Timothy Josling
April 1998   ISBN 0-88132-256-3

54 Real Exchange Rates for the Year 2000
Simon Wren Lewis and Rebecca Driver
April 1998   ISBN 0-88132-253-9

55 The Asian Financial Crisis: Causes, Cures,
and Systemic Implications
Morris Goldstein
June 1998   ISBN 0-88132-261-X

56 Global Economic Effects of the Asian
Currency Devaluations   Marcus Noland,
LiGang Liu, Sherman Robinson, and Zhi
Wang
July 1998   ISBN 0-88132-260-1

57 The Exchange Stabilization Fund: Slush
Money or War Chest?   C. Randall Henning
May 1999   ISBN 0-88132-271-7

58 The New Politics of American Trade:
Trade, Labor, and the Environment
I. M. Destler and Peter J. Balint
October 1999   ISBN 0-88132-269-5

59 Congressional Trade Votes: From NAFTA
Approval to Fast Track Defeat
Robert E. Baldwin and Christopher S. Magee
February 2000   ISBN 0-88132-267-9

60 Exchange Rate Regimes for Emerging
Markets: Reviving the Intermediate Option
John Williamson
September 2000   ISBN 0-88132-293-8

61 NAFTA and the Environment: Seven Years
Later   Gary Clyde Hufbauer, Daniel Esty,
Diana Orejas, Luis Rubio, and Jeffrey J.
Schott
October 2000   ISBN 0-88132-299-7

62 Free Trade between Korea and the United
States?   Inbom Choi and Jeffrey J. Schott
April 2001   ISBN 0-88132-311-X

63 New Regional Trading Arrangements in
the Asia Pacific?   Robert Scollay and
John P. Gilbert
May 2001   ISBN 0-88132-302-0

64 Parental Supervision: The New Paradigm
for Foreign Direct Investment and
Development   Theodore H. Moran
August 2001   ISBN 0-88132-313-6

65 The Benefits of Price Convergence:
Speculative Calculations
Gary Clyde Hufbauer, Erika Wada, and
Tony Warren
December 2001   ISBN 0-88132-333-0

66 Managed Floating Plus   Morris Goldstein
March 2002   ISBN 0-88132-336-5

67 Argentina and the Fund: From Triumph to
Tragedy   Michael Mussa
July 2002   ISBN 0-88132-339-X

68 East Asian Financial Cooperation
C. Randall Henning
September 2002   ISBN 0-88132-338-1

69 Reforming OPIC for the 21st Century
Theodore H. Moran
May 2003   ISBN 0-88132-342-X

70 Awakening Monster: The Alien Tort
Statute of 1789   Gary Clyde Hufbauer and
Nicholas Mitrokostas
July 2003   ISBN 0-88132-366-7

71 Korea after Kim Jong-il   Marcus Noland
January 2004   ISBN 0-88132-373-X

72 Roots of Competitiveness: China's
Evolving Agriculture Interests
Daniel H. Rosen, Scott Rozelle, and Jikun
Huang
July 2004   ISBN 0-88132-376-4

73 Prospects for a US-Taiwan FTA
Nicholas R. Lardy and Daniel H. Rosen
December 2004   ISBN 0-88132-367-5

74 Anchoring Reform with a US-Egypt Free
Trade Agreement   Ahmed Galal and
Robert Z. Lawrence
April 2005   ISBN 0-88132-368-3

75 Curbing the Boom-Bust Cycle: Stabilizing
Capital Flows to Emerging Markets
John Williamson
July 2005   ISBN 0-88132-330-6

76 The Shape of a Swiss-US Free Trade
Agreement   Gary Clyde Hufbauer and
Richard E. Baldwin
February 2006   ISBN 978-0-88132-385-6

77 A Strategy for IMF Reform
Edwin M. Truman
February 2006   ISBN 978-0-88132-398-6

78 US-China Trade Disputes: Rising Tide,
Rising Stakes   Gary Clyde Hufbauer,
Yee Wong, and Ketki Sheth
August 2006   ISBN 978-0-88132-394-8

79 Trade Relations Between Colombia and
the United States   Jeffrey J. Schott, ed.
August 2006   ISBN 978-0-88132-389-4

80 Sustaining Reform with a US-Pakistan
Free Trade Agreement
Gary Clyde Hufbauer and Shahid Javed
Burki
November 2006   ISBN 978-0-88132-395-5

81 A US–Middle East Trade Agreement: A
Circle of Opportunity?
Robert Z. Lawrence
November 2006   ISBN 978-0-88132-396-2

82 Reference Rates and the International
Monetary System   John Williamson
January 2007   ISBN 978-0-88132-401-3

83 Toward a US-Indonesia Free Trade
Agreement   Gary Clyde Hufbauer and
Sjamsu Rahardja
June 2007   ISBN 978-0-88132-402-0

84 The Accelerating Decline in America's
    High-Skilled Workforce
    Jacob Funk Kirkegaard
    December 2007   ISBN 978-0-88132-413-6
85 Blue-Collar Blues: Is Trade to Blame for
    Rising US Income Inequality?
    Robert Z. Lawrence
    January 2008   ISBN 978-0-88132-414-3
86 Maghreb Regional and Global Integration:
    A Dream to Be Fulfilled
    Gary Clyde Hufbauer and Claire Brunel, eds.
    October 2008   ISBN 978-0-88132-426-6
87 The Future of China's Exchange Rate
    Policy   Morris Goldstein and
    Nicholas R. Lardy
    July 2009   ISBN 978-0-88132-416-7
88 Capitalizing on the Morocco-US Free
    Trade Agreement: A Road Map for Success
    Gary Clyde Hufbauer and Claire Brunel, eds
    September 2009   ISBN 978-0-88132-433-4
89 Three Threats: An Analytical Framework
    for the CFIUS Process   Theodore H. Moran
    August 2009   ISBN 978-0-88132-429-7
90 Reengaging Egypt: Options for US-Egypt
    Economic Relations   Barbara Kotschwar and
    Jeffrey J. Schott
    January 2010   ISBN 978-088132-439-6
91 Figuring Out the Doha Round
    Gary Clyde Hufbauer, Jeffrey J. Schott, and
    Woan Foong Wong
    June 2010   ISBN 978-088132-503-4
92 China's Strategy to Secure Natural
    Resources: Risks, Dangers, and
    Opportunities   Theodore H. Moran
    June 2010   ISBN 978-088132-512-6
93 The Implications of China-Taiwan
    Economic Liberalization
    Daniel H. Rosen and Zhi Wang
    January 2011   ISBN 978-0-88132-501-0
94 The Global Outlook for Government Debt
    over the Next 25 Years: Implications for the
    Economy and Public Policy
    Joseph E. Gagnon with Marc
    Hinterschweiger
    June 2011   ISBN 978-0-88132-621-5
95 A Decade of Debt *(forthcoming)*
    Carmen M. Reinhart and Kenneth S. Rogoff
                ISBN 978-0-88132-621-5
96 Carbon Abatement Costs and Climate
    Change Finance   William R. Cline
    July 2010   ISBN 978-0-88132-607-9

BOOKS

IMF Conditionality*   John Williamson, ed.
1983   ISBN 0-88132-006-4
Trade Policy in the 1980s*   William R. Cline, ed.
1983   ISBN 0-88132-031-5
Subsidies in International Trade*
Gary Clyde Hufbauer and Joanna Shelton Erb
1984   ISBN 0-88132-004-8
International Debt: Systemic Risk and Policy
Response*   William R. Cline
1984   ISBN 0-88132-015-3

Trade Protection in the United States: 31 Case
Studies*   Gary Clyde Hufbauer,
Diane E. Berliner, and Kimberly Ann Elliott
1986   ISBN 0-88132-040-4
Toward Renewed Economic Growth in Latin
America*   Bela Balassa, Gerardo M. Bueno,
Pedro Pablo Kuczynski, and Mario Henrique
Simonsen
1986   ISBN 0-88132-045-5
Capital Flight and Third World Debt*
Donald R. Lessard and John Williamson, eds.
1987   ISBN 0-88132-053-6
The Canada-United States Free Trade
Agreement: The Global Impact*
Jeffrey J. Schott and Murray G. Smith, eds.
1988   ISBN 0-88132-073-0
World Agricultural Trade: Building a
Consensus*   William M. Miner and
Dale E. Hathaway, eds.
1988   ISBN 0-88132-071-3
Japan in the World Economy*   Bela Balassa and
Marcus Noland
1988   ISBN 0-88132-041-2
America in the World Economy: A Strategy
for the 1990s*   C. Fred Bergsten
1988   ISBN 0-88132-089-7
Managing the Dollar: From the Plaza to the
Louvre*   Yoichi Funabashi
1988, 2d ed. 1989   ISBN 0-88132-097-8
United States External Adjustment and the
World Economy*   William R. Cline
May 1989   ISBN 0-88132-048-X
Free Trade Areas and U.S. Trade Policy*
Jeffrey J. Schott, ed.
May 1989   ISBN 0-88132-094-3
Dollar Politics: Exchange Rate Policymaking
in the United States*   I. M. Destler and
C. Randall Henning
September 1989   ISBN 0-88132-079-X
Latin American Adjustment: How Much Has
Happened?*   John Williamson, ed.
April 1990   ISBN 0-88132-125-7
The Future of World Trade in Textiles and
Apparel*   William R. Cline
1987, 2d ed. June 1999   ISBN 0-88132-110-9
Completing the Uruguay Round: A Results-
Oriented Approach to the GATT Trade
Negotiations*   Jeffrey J. Schott, ed.
September 1990   ISBN 0-88132-130-3
Economic Sanctions Reconsidered (2 volumes)
Economic Sanctions Reconsidered:
Supplemental Case Histories
Gary Clyde Hufbauer, Jeffrey J. Schott, and
Kimberly Ann Elliott
1985, 2d ed. Dec. 1990 ISBN cloth 0-88132-115-X
                ISBN paper 0-88132-105-2
Economic Sanctions Reconsidered: History
and Current Policy   Gary Clyde Hufbauer,
Jeffrey J. Schott, and Kimberly Ann Elliott
December 1990   ISBN cloth 0-88132-140-0
                ISBN paper 0-88132-136-2

Pacific Basin Developing Countries: Prospects
for the Future*   Marcus Noland
January 1991   ISBN cloth 0-88132-141-9
                       ISBN paper 0-88132-081-1
Currency Convertibility in Eastern Europe*
John Williamson, ed.
October 1991   ISBN 0-88132-128-1
International Adjustment and Financing: The
Lessons of 1985-1991*   C. Fred Bergsten, ed.
January 1992   ISBN 0-88132-112-5
North American Free Trade: Issues and
Recommendations*   Gary Clyde Hufbauer and
Jeffrey J. Schott
April 1992   ISBN 0-88132-120-6
Narrowing the U.S. Current Account Deficit*
Alan J. Lenz
June 1992   ISBN 0-88132-103-6
The Economics of Global Warming
William R. Cline
June 1992   ISBN 0-88132-132-X
US Taxation of International Income:
Blueprint for Reform   Gary Clyde Hufbauer,
assisted by Joanna M. van Rooij
October 1992   ISBN 0-88132-134-6
Who's Bashing Whom? Trade Conflict in High-
Technology Industries   Laura D'Andrea Tyson
November 1992   ISBN 0-88132-106-0
Korea in the World Economy*   Il SaKong
January 1993   ISBN 0-88132-183-4
Pacific Dynamism and the International
Economic System*   C. Fred Bergsten and
Marcus Noland, eds.
May 1993   ISBN 0-88132-196-6
Economic Consequences of Soviet
Disintegration*   John Williamson, ed.
May 1993   ISBN 0-88132-190-7
Reconcilable Differences? United States-Japan
Economic Conflict*   C. Fred Bergsten and
Marcus Noland
June 1993   ISBN 0-88132-129-X
Does Foreign Exchange Intervention Work?
Kathryn M. Dominguez and Jeffrey A. Frankel
September 1993   ISBN 0-88132-104-4
Sizing Up U.S. Export Disincentives*
J. David Richardson
September 1993   ISBN 0-88132-107-9
NAFTA: An Assessment
Gary Clyde Hufbauer and Jeffrey J. Schott, *rev. ed.*
October 1993   ISBN 0-88132-199-0
Adjusting to Volatile Energy Prices
Philip K. Verleger, Jr.
November 1993   ISBN 0-88132-069-2
The Political Economy of Policy Reform
John Williamson, ed.
January 1994   ISBN 0-88132-195-8
Measuring the Costs of Protection in the
United States   Gary Clyde Hufbauer and
Kimberly Ann Elliott
January 1994   ISBN 0-88132-108-7
The Dynamics of Korean Economic
Development*   Cho Soon
March 1994   ISBN 0-88132-162-1

Reviving the European Union*
C. Randall Henning, Eduard Hochreiter, and
Gary Clyde Hufbauer, eds.
April 1994   ISBN 0-88132-208-3
China in the World Economy
Nicholas R. Lardy
April 1994   ISBN 0-88132-200-8
Greening the GATT: Trade, Environment,
and the Future   Daniel C. Esty
July 1994   ISBN 0-88132-205-9
Western Hemisphere Economic Integration*
Gary Clyde Hufbauer and Jeffrey J. Schott
July 1994   ISBN 0-88132-159-1
Currencies and Politics in the United States,
Germany, and Japan   C. Randall Henning
September 1994   ISBN 0-88132-127-3
Estimating Equilibrium Exchange Rates
John Williamson, ed.
September 1994   ISBN 0-88132-076-5
Managing the World Economy: Fifty Years
after Bretton Woods   Peter B. Kenen, ed.
September 1994   ISBN 0-88132-212-1
Reciprocity and Retaliation in U.S. Trade
Policy   Thomas O. Bayard and
Kimberly Ann Elliott
September 1994   ISBN 0-88132-084-6
The Uruguay Round: An Assessment*
Jeffrey J. Schott, assisted by Johanna Buurman
November 1994   ISBN 0-88132-206-7
Measuring the Costs of Protection in Japan*
Yoko Sazanami, Shujiro Urata, and Hiroki Kawai
January 1995   ISBN 0-88132-211-3
Foreign Direct Investment in the United States,
3d ed.   Edward M. Graham and
Paul R. Krugman
January 1995   ISBN 0-88132-204-0
The Political Economy of Korea-United States
Cooperation*   C. Fred Bergsten and
Il SaKong, eds.
February 1995   ISBN 0-88132-213-X
International Debt Reexamined*
William R. Cline
February 1995   ISBN 0-88132-083-8
American Trade Politics, 3d ed.   I. M. Destler
April 1995   ISBN 0-88132-215-6
Managing Official Export Credits: The Quest
for a Global Regime*   John E. Ray
July 1995   ISBN 0-88132-207-5
Asia Pacific Fusion: Japan's Role in APEC*
Yoichi Funabashi
October 1995   ISBN 0-88132-224-5
Korea-United States Cooperation in the New
World Order*   C. Fred Bergsten and
Il SaKong, eds.
February 1996   ISBN 0-88132-226-1
Why Exports Really Matter!*
                           ISBN 0-88132-221-0
Why Exports Matter More!* ISBN 0-88132-229-6
J. David Richardson and Karin Rindal
July 1995; February 1996
Global Corporations and National
Governments   Edward M. Graham
May 1996   ISBN 0-88132-111-7

Global Economic Leadership and the Group of
Seven   C. Fred Bergsten and
C. Randall Henning
May 1996   ISBN 0-88132-218-0
The Trading System after the Uruguay Round*
John Whalley and Colleen Hamilton
July 1996   ISBN 0-88132-131-1
Private Capital Flows to Emerging Markets
after the Mexican Crisis*   Guillermo A. Calvo,
Morris Goldstein, and Eduard Hochreiter
September 1996   ISBN 0-88132-232-6
The Crawling Band as an Exchange Rate
Regime: Lessons from Chile, Colombia, and
Israel   John Williamson
September 1996   ISBN 0-88132-231-8
Flying High: Liberalizing Civil Aviation in the
Asia Pacific*   Gary Clyde Hufbauer and
Christopher Findlay
November 1996   ISBN 0-88132-227-X
Measuring the Costs of Visible Protection
in Korea*   Namdoo Kim
November 1996   ISBN 0-88132-236-9
The World Trading System: Challenges Ahead
Jeffrey J. Schott
December 1996   ISBN 0-88132-235-0
Has Globalization Gone Too Far?   Dani Rodrik
March 1997   ISBN paper 0-88132-241-5
Korea-United States Economic Relationship*
C. Fred Bergsten and Il SaKong, eds.
March 1997   ISBN 0-88132-240-7
Summitry in the Americas: A Progress Report
Richard E. Feinberg
April 1997   ISBN 0-88132-242-3
Corruption and the Global Economy
Kimberly Ann Elliott
June 1997   ISBN 0-88132-233-4
Regional Trading Blocs in the World Economic
System   Jeffrey A. Frankel
October 1997   ISBN 0-88132-202-4
Sustaining the Asia Pacific Miracle:
Environmental Protection and Economic
Integration   Andre Dua and Daniel C. Esty
October 1997   ISBN 0-88132-250-4
Trade and Income Distribution
William R. Cline
November 1997   ISBN 0-88132-216-4
Global Competition Policy
Edward M. Graham and J. David Richardson
December 1997   ISBN 0-88132-166-4
Unfinished Business: Telecommunications
after the Uruguay Round
Gary Clyde Hufbauer and Erika Wada
December 1997   ISBN 0-88132-257-1
Financial Services Liberalization in the WTO
Wendy Dobson and Pierre Jacquet
June 1998   ISBN 0-88132-254-7
Restoring Japan's Economic Growth
Adam S. Posen
September 1998   ISBN 0-88132-262-8
Measuring the Costs of Protection in China
Zhang Shuguang, Zhang Yansheng, and Wan
Zhongxin
November 1998   ISBN 0-88132-247-4

Foreign Direct Investment and Development:
The New Policy Agenda for Developing
Countries and Economies in Transition
Theodore H. Moran
December 1998   ISBN 0-88132-258-X
Behind the Open Door: Foreign Enterprises
in the Chinese Marketplace   Daniel H. Rosen
January 1999   ISBN 0-88132-263-6
Toward A New International Financial
Architecture: A Practical Post-Asia Agenda
Barry Eichengreen
February 1999   ISBN 0-88132-270-9
Is the U.S. Trade Deficit Sustainable?
Catherine L. Mann
September 1999   ISBN 0-88132-265-2
Safeguarding Prosperity in a Global Financial
System: The Future International Financial
Architecture, Independent Task Force Report
Sponsored by the Council on Foreign Relations
Morris Goldstein, Project Director
October 1999   ISBN 0-88132-287-3
Avoiding the Apocalypse: The Future of the
Two Koreas   Marcus Noland
June 2000   ISBN 0-88132-278-4
Assessing Financial Vulnerability: An Early
Warning System for Emerging Markets
Morris Goldstein, Graciela Kaminsky, and
Carmen Reinhart
June 2000   ISBN 0-88132-237-7
Global Electronic Commerce: A Policy Primer
Catherine L. Mann, Sue E. Eckert, and Sarah
Cleeland Knight
July 2000   ISBN 0-88132-274-1
The WTO after Seattle   Jeffrey J. Schott, ed.
July 2000   ISBN 0-88132-290-3
Intellectual Property Rights in the Global
Economy   Keith E. Maskus
August 2000   ISBN 0-88132-282-2
The Political Economy of the Asian Financial
Crisis   Stephan Haggard
August 2000   ISBN 0-88132-283-0
Transforming Foreign Aid: United States
Assistance in the 21st Century   Carol Lancaster
August 2000   ISBN 0-88132-291-1
Fighting the Wrong Enemy: Antiglobal
Activists and Multinational Enterprises
Edward M. Graham
September 2000   ISBN 0-88132-272-5
Globalization and the Perceptions of American
Workers   Kenneth Scheve and
Matthew J. Slaughter
March 2001   ISBN 0-88132-295-4
World Capital Markets: Challenge to the G-10
Wendy Dobson and Gary Clyde Hufbauer,
assisted by Hyun Koo Cho
May 2001   ISBN 0-88132-301-2
Prospects for Free Trade in the Americas
Jeffrey J. Schott
August 2001   ISBN 0-88132-275-X
Toward a North American Community:
Lessons from the Old World for the New
Robert A. Pastor
August 2001   ISBN 0-88132-328-4

Measuring the Costs of Protection in Europe:
European Commercial Policy in the 2000s
Patrick A. Messerlin
September 2001   ISBN 0-88132-273-3
Job Loss from Imports: Measuring the Costs
Lori G. Kletzer
September 2001   ISBN 0-88132-296-2
No More Bashing: Building a New Japan–
United States Economic Relationship
C. Fred Bergsten, Takatoshi Ito, and Marcus
Noland
October 2001   ISBN 0-88132-286-5
Why Global Commitment Really Matters!
Howard Lewis III and J. David Richardson
October 2001   ISBN 0-88132-298-9
Leadership Selection in the Major Multilaterals
Miles Kahler
November 2001   ISBN 0-88132-335-7
The International Financial Architecture:
What's New? What's Missing?   Peter B. Kenen
November 2001   ISBN 0-88132-297-0
Delivering on Debt Relief: From IMF Gold to a
New Aid Architecture   John Williamson and
Nancy Birdsall, with Brian Deese
April 2002   ISBN 0-88132-331-4
Imagine There's No Country: Poverty,
Inequality, and Growth in the Era of
Globalization   Surjit S. Bhalla
September 2002   ISBN 0-88132-348-9
Reforming Korea's Industrial Conglomerates
Edward M. Graham
January 2003   ISBN 0-88132-337-3
Industrial Policy in an Era of Globalization:
Lessons from Asia   Marcus Noland and
Howard Pack
March 2003   ISBN 0-88132-350-0
Reintegrating India with the World Economy
T. N. Srinivasan and Suresh D. Tendulkar
March 2003   ISBN 0-88132-280-6
After the Washington Consensus: Restarting
Growth and Reform in Latin America
Pedro-Pablo Kuczynski and John Williamson, eds.
March 2003   ISBN 0-88132-347-0
The Decline of US Labor Unions and the Role
of Trade   Robert E. Baldwin
June 2003   ISBN 0-88132-341-1
Can Labor Standards Improve under
Globalization?   Kimberly Ann Elliott and
Richard B. Freeman
June 2003   ISBN 0-88132-332-2
Crimes and Punishments? Retaliation under
the WTO   Robert Z. Lawrence
October 2003   ISBN 0-88132-359-4
Inflation Targeting in the World Economy
Edwin M. Truman
October 2003   ISBN 0-88132-345-4
Foreign Direct Investment and Tax
Competition   John H. Mutti
November 2003   ISBN 0-88132-352-7
Has Globalization Gone Far Enough? The
Costs of Fragmented Markets
Scott C. Bradford and Robert Z. Lawrence
February 2004   ISBN 0-88132-349-7

Food Regulation and Trade: Toward a Safe and
Open Global System   Tim Josling,
Donna Roberts, and David Orden
March 2004   ISBN 0-88132-346-2
Controlling Currency Mismatches in Emerging
Markets   Morris Goldstein and Philip Turner
April 2004   ISBN 0-88132-360-8
Free Trade Agreements: US Strategies and
Priorities   Jeffrey J. Schott, ed.
April 2004   ISBN 0-88132-361-6
Trade Policy and Global Poverty
William R. Cline
June 2004   ISBN 0-88132-365-9
Bailouts or Bail-ins? Responding to Financial
Crises in Emerging Economies
Nouriel Roubini and Brad Setser
August 2004   ISBN 0-88132-371-3
Transforming the European Economy
Martin Neil Baily and Jacob Funk Kirkegaard
September 2004   ISBN 0-88132-343-8
Chasing Dirty Money: The Fight Against
Money Laundering   Peter Reuter and
Edwin M. Truman
November 2004   ISBN 0-88132-370-5
The United States and the World Economy:
Foreign Economic Policy for the Next Decade
C. Fred Bergsten
January 2005   ISBN 0-88132-380-2
Does Foreign Direct Investment Promote
Development?   Theodore H. Moran,
Edward M. Graham, and Magnus Blomström,
eds.
April 2005   ISBN 0-88132-381-0
American Trade Politics, 4th ed.   I. M. Destler
June 2005   ISBN 0-88132-382-9
Why Does Immigration Divide America?
Public Finance and Political Opposition to
Open Borders   Gordon H. Hanson
August 2005   ISBN 0-88132-400-0
Reforming the US Corporate Tax
Gary Clyde Hufbauer and Paul L. E. Grieco
September 2005   ISBN 0-88132-384-5
The United States as a Debtor Nation
William R. Cline
September 2005   ISBN 0-88132-399-3
NAFTA Revisited: Achievements and
Challenges   Gary Clyde Hufbauer and
Jeffrey J. Schott, assisted by Paul L. E. Grieco and
Yee Wong
October 2005   ISBN 0-88132-334-9
US National Security and Foreign Direct
Investment   Edward M. Graham and
David M. Marchick
May 2006   ISBN 978-0-88132-391-7
Accelerating the Globalization of America: The
Role for Information Technology
Catherine L. Mann, assisted by Jacob Funk
Kirkegaard
June 2006   ISBN 978-0-88132-390-0
Delivering on Doha: Farm Trade and the Poor
Kimberly Ann Elliott
July 2006   ISBN 978-0-88132-392-4

Case Studies in US Trade Negotiation, Vol. 1:
Making the Rules   Charan Devereaux,
Robert Z. Lawrence, and Michael Watkins
September 2006   ISBN 978-0-88132-362-7
Case Studies in US Trade Negotiation, Vol. 2:
Resolving Disputes   Charan Devereaux,
Robert Z. Lawrence, and Michael Watkins
September 2006   ISBN 978-0-88132-363-2
C. Fred Bergsten and the World Economy
Michael Mussa, ed.
December 2006   ISBN 978-0-88132-397-9
Working Papers, Volume I   Peterson Institute
December 2006   ISBN 978-0-88132-388-7
The Arab Economies in a Changing World
Marcus Noland and Howard Pack
April 2007   ISBN 978-0-88132-393-1
Working Papers, Volume II   Peterson Institute
April 2007   ISBN 978-0-88132-404-4
Global Warming and Agriculture: Impact
Estimates by Country   William R. Cline
July 2007   ISBN 978-0-88132-403-7
US Taxation of Foreign Income
Gary Clyde Hufbauer and Ariel Assa
October 2007   ISBN 978-0-88132-405-1
Russia's Capitalist Revolution: Why Market
Reform Succeeded and Democracy Failed
Anders Åslund
October 2007   ISBN 978-0-88132-409-9
Economic Sanctions Reconsidered, 3d ed.
Gary Clyde Hufbauer, Jeffrey J. Schott, Kimberly
Ann Elliott, and Barbara Oegg
November 2007
          ISBN hardcover 978-0-88132-407-5
    ISBN hardcover/CD-ROM 978-0-88132-408-2
Debating China's Exchange Rate Policy
Morris Goldstein and Nicholas R. Lardy, eds.
April 2008   ISBN 978-0-88132-415-0
Leveling the Carbon Playing Field:
International Competition and US Climate
Policy Design   Trevor Houser, Rob Bradley, Britt
Childs, Jacob Werksman, and Robert Heilmayr
May 2008   ISBN 978-0-88132-420-4
Accountability and Oversight of US Exchange
Rate Policy   C. Randall Henning
June 2008   ISBN 978-0-88132-419-8
Challenges of Globalization: Imbalances and
Growth   Anders Åslund and
Marek Dabrowski, eds.
July 2008   ISBN 978-0-88132-418-1
China's Rise: Challenges and Opportunities
C. Fred Bergsten, Charles Freeman, Nicholas R.
Lardy, and Derek J. Mitchell
September 2008   ISBN 978-0-88132-417-4
Banking on Basel: The Future of International
Financial Regulation   Daniel K. Tarullo
September 2008   ISBN 978-0-88132-423-5
US Pension Reform: Lessons from Other
Countries   Martin Neil Baily and
Jacob Funk Kirkegaard
February 2009   ISBN 978-0-88132-425-9
How Ukraine Became a Market Economy and
Democracy   Anders Åslund
March 2009   ISBN 978-0-88132-427-3

Global Warming and the World Trading
System   Gary Clyde Hufbauer,
Steve Charnovitz, and Jisun Kim
March 2009   ISBN 978-0-88132-428-0
The Russia Balance Sheet   Anders Åslund and
Andrew Kuchins
March 2009   ISBN 978-0-88132-424-2
The Euro at Ten: The Next Global Currency?
Jean Pisani-Ferry and Adam S. Posen, eds.
July 2009   ISBN 978-0-88132-430-3
Financial Globalization, Economic Growth, and
the Crisis of 2007–09   William R. Cline
May 2010   ISBN 978-0-88132-4990-0
Russia after the Global Economic Crisis
Anders Åslund, Sergei Guriev, and Andrew
Kuchins, eds.
June 2010   ISBN 978-0-88132-497-6
Sovereign Wealth Funds: Threat or Salvation?
Edwin M. Truman
September 2010   ISBN 978-0-88132-498-3
The Last Shall Be the First: The East European
Financial Crisis, 2008–10   Anders Åslund
October 2010   ISBN 978-0-88132-521-8
Witness to Transformation: Refugee Insights
into North Korea   Stephan Haggard and
Marcus Noland
January 2011   ISBN 978-0-88132-438-9
Foreign Direct Investment and Development:
Launching a Second Generation of Policy
Research, Avoiding the Mistakes of the First,
Reevaluating Policies for Developed and
Developing Countries   Theodore H. Moran
April 2011   ISBN 978-0-88132-600-0
How Latvia Came through the Financial Crisis
Anders Åslund and Valdis Dombrovskis
May 2011   ISBN 978-0-88132-602-4

SPECIAL REPORTS

1   Promoting World Recovery: A Statement
     on Global Economic Strategy*
     by 26 Economists from Fourteen Countries
     December 1982   ISBN 0-88132-013-7
2   Prospects for Adjustment in Argentina,
     Brazil, and Mexico: Responding to the
     Debt Crisis*   John Williamson, ed.
     June 1983   ISBN 0-88132-016-1
3   Inflation and Indexation: Argentina, Brazil,
     and Israel*   John Williamson, ed.
     March 1985   ISBN 0-88132-037-4
4   Global Economic Imbalances*
     C. Fred Bergsten, ed.
     March 1986   ISBN 0-88132-042-0
5   African Debt and Financing*
     Carol Lancaster and John Williamson, eds.
     May 1986   ISBN 0-88132-044-7
6   Resolving the Global Economic Crisis:
     After Wall Street*   by Thirty-three
     Economists from Thirteen Countries
     December 1987   ISBN 0-88132-070-6
7   World Economic Problems*
     Kimberly Ann Elliott and John Williamson,
     eds.
     April 1988   ISBN 0-88132-055-2

Reforming World Agricultural Trade*
by Twenty-nine Professionals from
Seventeen Countries
1988   ISBN 0-88132-088-9
8   Economic Relations Between the United
States and Korea: Conflict or Cooperation?*
Thomas O. Bayard and Soogil Young, eds.
January 1989   ISBN 0-88132-068-4
9   Whither APEC? The Progress to Date and
Agenda for the Future*
C. Fred Bergsten, ed.
October 1997   ISBN 0-88132-248-2
10   Economic Integration of the Korean
Peninsula   Marcus Noland, ed.
January 1998   ISBN 0-88132-255-5
11   Restarting Fast Track*   Jeffrey J. Schott, ed.
April 1998   ISBN 0-88132-259-8
12   Launching New Global Trade Talks: An
Action Agenda   Jeffrey J. Schott, ed.
September 1998   ISBN 0-88132-266-0
13   Japan's Financial Crisis and Its Parallels to
US Experience   Ryoichi Mikitani and
Adam S. Posen, eds.
September 2000   ISBN 0-88132-289-X
14   The Ex-Im Bank in the 21st Century: A
New Approach   Gary Clyde Hufbauer and
Rita M. Rodriguez, eds.
January 2001   ISBN 0-88132-300-4
15   The Korean Diaspora in the World
Economy   C. Fred Bergsten and
Inbom Choi, eds.
January 2003   ISBN 0-88132-358-6
16   Dollar Overvaluation and the World
Economy   C. Fred Bergsten and
John Williamson, eds.
February 2003   ISBN 0-88132-351-9
17   Dollar Adjustment: How Far? Against
What?   C. Fred Bergsten and
John Williamson, eds.
November 2004   ISBN 0-88132-378-0
18   The Euro at Five: Ready for a Global Role?
Adam S. Posen, ed.
April 2005   ISBN 0-88132-380-2
19   Reforming the IMF for the 21st Century
Edwin M. Truman, ed.
April 2006   ISBN 978-0-88132-387-0

20   The Long-Term International Economic
Position of the United States
C. Fred Bergsten, ed.
May 2009   ISBN 978-0-88132-432-7

WORKS IN PROGRESS

China's Energy Evolution: The Consequences
of Powering Growth at Home and Abroad
Daniel H. Rosen and Trevor Houser
Global Identity Theft: Economic and Policy
Implications   Catherine L. Mann
Globalized Venture Capital: Implications
for US Entrepreneurship and Innovation
Catherine L. Mann
Forging a Grand Bargain: Expanding Trade and
Raising Worker Prosperity   Lori G. Kletzer,
J. David Richardson, and Howard F. Rosen
Why Reform a Rich Country? Germany and the
Future of Capitalism   Adam S. Posen
Global Forces, American Faces: US Economic
Globalization at the Grass Roots
J. David Richardson
The Impact of Global Services Outsourcing on
American Firms and Workers J. Bradford Jensen
Policy Reform in Rich Countries
John Williamson, ed.
Banking System Fragility in Emerging
Economies   Morris Goldstein and Philip Turner
Aligning NAFTA with Climate Change
Objectives   Meera Fickling and
Jeffrey J. Schott
Private Rights and Public Problems: The
Global Economics of Intellectual Property in
the 21st Century   Keith Maskus
The Positive Agenda for Climate Change and
Trade   Trevor Houser, Jacob Funk Kirkegaard,
and Rob Bradley
Stable Prices, Unstable Currencies: The Weak
Link between Exchange Rates and Inflation
and What It Means for Economic Policy
Joseph E. Gagnon

DISTRIBUTORS OUTSIDE THE UNITED STATES

**Australia, New Zealand,
and Papua New Guinea**
D. A. Information Services
648 Whitehorse Road
Mitcham, Victoria 3132, Australia
Tel: 61-3-9210-7777
Fax: 61-3-9210-7788
Email: service@dadirect.com.au
www.dadirect.com.au

India, Bangladesh, Nepal, and Sri Lanka
Viva Books Private Limited
Mr. Vinod Vasishtha
4737/23 Ansari Road
Daryaganj, New Delhi 110002
India
Tel: 91-11-4224-2200
Fax: 91-11-4224-2240
Email: viva@vivagroupindia.net
www.vivagroupindia.com

**Mexico, Central America, South America,
and Puerto Rico**
US PubRep, Inc.
311 Dean Drive
Rockville, MD 20851
Tel: 301-838-9276
Fax: 301-838-9278
Email: c.falk@ieee.org

**Asia (*Brunei, Burma, Cambodia, China,
Hong Kong, Indonesia, Korea, Laos, Malaysia,
Philippines, Singapore, Taiwan, Thailand,
and Vietnam*)**
East-West Export Books (EWEB)
University of Hawaii Press
2840 Kolowalu Street
Honolulu, Hawaii 96822-1888
Tel: 808-956-8830
Fax: 808-988-6052
Email: eweb@hawaii.edu

Canada
Renouf Bookstore
5369 Canotek Road, Unit 1
Ottawa, Ontario KlJ 9J3, Canada
Tel: 613-745-2665
Fax: 613-745-7660
www.renoufbooks.com

Japan
United Publishers Services Ltd.
1-32-5, Higashi-shinagawa
Shinagawa-ku, Tokyo 140-0002
Japan
Tel: 81-3-5479-7251
Fax: 81-3-5479-7307
Email: purchasing@ups.co.jp
*For trade accounts only. Individuals will find
Institute books in leading Tokyo bookstores.*

Middle East
MERIC
2 Bahgat Ali Street, El Masry Towers
Tower D, Apt. 24
Zamalek, Cairo
Egypt
Tel. 20-2-7633824
Fax: 20-2-7369355
Email: mahmoud_fouda@mericonline.com
www.mericonline.com

**United Kingdom, Europe
(*including Russia and Turkey*), Africa,
and Israel**
The Eurospan Group
c/o Turpin Distribution
Pegasus Drive
Stratton Business Park
Biggleswade, Bedfordshire
SG18 8TQ
United Kingdom
Tel: 44 (0) 1767-604972
Fax: 44 (0) 1767-601640
Email: eurospan@turpin-distribution.com
www.eurospangroup.com/bookstore

**Visit our website at:
www.piie.com
E-mail orders to:
petersonmail@presswarehouse.com**